Glorious Adventure

Discovering the Treasure of Taking Christ to the Nations

By: Phillip Douglas

Printed in the United States of America.

Praise for *Glorious Adventure*:

"We Christians have received the four Gospels, Matthew, Mark, Luke, and John. However, every baptized person who has become a missionary disciple of Christ has to write or compose a fifth Gospel. Here is one fifth Gospel of the Douglas family. These pure, simple, gentle, and true stories inspired through the work of the Holy Spirit are both restless, bold, brazen and courageous on the one hand, and yet honest, candid and persuasive on the other hand. With the Douglas family, and all the readers of this book, I pray that the missionary zeal will flood the Church and all the baptized and confirmed."

- Rt. Reverend Anonymous Bishop, Asia

"Some of the most wonderful things happening in the Catholic Church today are as yet not widely known. But all over the world the Holy Spirit has been working to raise up pockets of fervent Christian life out of which great fruit is being borne. One of these unknown wonders is the existence of Family Missions Company. Based in Louisiana, for many years now hundreds of families and single people have been going to the far corners of the world to bring Jesus and his gospel to those who need him. This book tells the inspiring story of one such family who as they came to grips with the call of Jesus to come follow him, left their friends and relatives and their pursuit of the American Dream to live as radical disciples of Jesus. The book is very well written and honestly tells the story of this family's struggles as well as their triumphs and their continuing effort to be faithful to the call. As one reads the book however one becomes aware that this is a call which all of us have received and which each of us needs to discern what it means for our own lives. A very inspiring book and well worth reading."

- Dr. Ralph Martin, S.T.D. Founder of Renewal Ministries

"Phillip and his family are extraordinary witnesses for Christ. They took a bold leap to follow God's plan for their life and in doing so found the abundance God promised. In *Glorious Adventure* Phillip invites us to live passionately, courageously and trust God with everything. Do you want to take the next step in your faith and find lasting purpose and joy? If so, this book is for you.

- Paul George, Author *Rethink Happiness*

"I wept tears of joy and conviction as I read Phil's life-changing book. Filled with courageous passion that cries out for total transformation of every Christian heart, *Glorious Adventure* breaks open Scripture and the words of the Saints to illustrate what it really means to follow Jesus wholeheartedly. Phil and Lacy's experience of going into foreign missions with their six children provides an abundance of powerful stories, woven together into a captivating page turner I just couldn't put down! I know you will enjoy *Glorious Adventure*, and I pray that you will be forever changed."

-Sarah Summers Granger, Executive Director, Family Missions Company

Table of Contents

Acknowledgments

This book has been a work in progress over the last couple of years and was written in five different countries, on two hemispheres, and on three different computers, two of which bit the dust in the line of duty. From rickshaws too small to fit our entire family, to dirt roads leading to nowhere, this story has truly seen it all.

I want to thank my amazing and beautiful wife, Lacy, who committed her life to Jesus long before she committed herself to marrying me. Your faithfulness and willingness to follow Jesus across the world bringing the hope of the Gospel to so many in need while still being an amazing wife and mothering our children with such grace is inspiring.

A huge thank you to our children, whose yes to follow Jesus as world missionaries has been astounding. You traded private schools and your private bedrooms for home-school with your parents and a spirit of *we share everything*. We are so proud of you! I wonder if we will all get to share rooms together in heaven. I sure hope so. Your smiles and authentic zest for living an abundant life (John 10:10) have opened up hundreds of doors for the light of Christ to come pouring through. What an amazing adventure! You will be rewarded greatly in this life and in the life to come.

A special and important thank you goes to the many family members, friends, and benefactors who have generously supported, and who are still generously supporting our family's mission. Your love, prayers, and monetary support are the fuel that keeps us in this race. As you know, we truly could not be serving God in this capacity without you.

This book is dedicated to the hundreds of faithful and radical missionaries serving with Family Missions Company. You are all a witness to our family of what radical missionary discipleship looks like. You are all our friends, yet you are our heroes. We could never repay you for your inspiration and encouragement along this amazing adventure.

And finally, this book belongs to the many beautiful people whom God has placed before us in our life of service as missionaries. You have served us far more than we have served you. We may have found some of you poor, lost, and unreached on the outside, but we have seen the image and likeness of God in each one of you. Thank you.

"I have come that they may have life and have it more abundantly."

- John 10:10

Introduction

"The kingdom of heaven is like a treasure buried in a field, which a person finds and hides again, and out of joy goes and sells all that he has and buys that field."

– Matthew 13:44

A few years back, our family's life was completely redirected. We were living a great and blessed life in suburban America, doing our very best to follow Jesus and serve Him and others in the Church and in our community. We briefly stepped outside of our usual surroundings to serve the poor and lost in rural Mexico. This is where God wrecked our plans, spun us around a few times, and then spit us back out filled with His Holy Spirit and a desire to bring Jesus Christ to the entire world. It has been a *Glorious Adventure*, and we have discovered a lifetime of new treasure along the way, treasure that lasts eternally.

With God's grace, I have been given so many new opportunities. I woke up this morning and felt my heart beating, a new opportunity. Jesus continues to run after me, offering me an endless opportunity of grace, love, and mercy. But who am I running after to introduce to Jesus Christ?

Jesus commands each of us to go to the ends of the earth with His Gospel, which is love. Yet far too often, we choose to remain within the comforts of our immediate surroundings.

You and I have an enormous role to play in fulfilling the Great Commission: to make disciples of all nations. Each one of us plays a vital and urgent role in taking Christ to the world. Our lives are passing us by at an insane pace, a pace that we cannot keep up with. As I grow older and see my children doing the same, I have come to this one conclusion: we are not here for very long, and our only purpose for being here is to know, love, and serve Jesus and wholeheartedly introduce Him and His infinite love to an entire world of lost, poor, and unreached people. That is it. Everything else I can do or dream up of doing (and there is a lot) is so far below this one purpose. *This* is the *Glorious Adventure* God is inviting us into each day.

There are roughly 7 billion people alive in the world today. It's an enormous world made up of vast cultures, religions, and languages, all created by God, our Father. Jesus Christ deeply desires us all. All seven billion.

My deepest prayer for anyone reading this book is that it will afford us all the time to die a bit more to ourselves in order to bring the hope of the resurrected Jesus Christ to a dying world. It's our only chance. Jesus is our only hope.

Oftentimes I feel like I may be the worst missionary God has ever called. I am weak, selfish, and oftentimes find myself wanting to look back. Perhaps you can relate? But when I focus on Jesus and not myself, I realize that all I am is a broken vessel asked to carry the Gospel and that Jesus is the only one who needs to have it all together. I rejoice in that and can find the strength for another day out here. Through our family's journey, from North America to Central America and finally to Asia, I hope that you will discover new and amazing ways that God is calling *you* to bring the goodness of the Gospel to the world. Oh that one day His name and renown would be the greatest treasure among all the nations!

Chapter 1: Erasing My American Dream

"And what you have is not Christianity at all, it's just some watered down Christian version of the American Dream."[1]

– Francis Chan

These were the words I had heard just a few years ago as I sat in my newly designed living room den after praying and reading early one morning. We had recently returned home from a week-long mission trip to a very rural town in northern Mexico. Our lives were undoubtedly changed forever. We had encountered the poor like never before, and for a week, we had evangelized door to door in small, dusty villages. We felt a small, fresh breeze inside of us that renewed us so much. We were parched; we were drained. I was working and chasing the American Dream.

As I sat on my large, overstuffed recliner with my enormous book collection surrounding me, I encountered this video by Francis Chan, and he was calling out all of American Christianity in one five-minute opportunity. He was challenging the Church to take risks, to live radically for Christ, and to allow God to hold the reins of our lives. He called me out as the poser I was becoming.

Sure, I was following Jesus, but was I living radically? Was the Holy Spirit guiding my life, or were my own desires guiding it? This short video had finalized the work that the Holy Spirit had already been doing in me since our Mexico trip, to go and selflessly make disciples of all nations. I longed to go so much deeper. I needed to do something, and I needed to do something fast.

But I was comfortable where I was, and I was a bit fearful. I felt somewhat like an overweight and selfish, boring, mediocre Christian stuck in my comfortable recliner watching life go by.

God was calling. Did I have the courage to follow Him?

But I'm not a bad person, and I am pretty involved at Church, too.

I can't tell you how many times I thought these words. I am embarrassed to write that. Is that the standard benchmark for being a fruitful Christian? Just don't be worse than most people around me and go to Church on Sundays?

To be honest, I was pretty involved in some ministries, and Lacy and I were neck-deep in raising our family. I worked long hours, and we were accumulating wealth. We had recently purchased our dream home, had a couple of great cars, retirement, businesses, investments, a boat, private schools, and a great marriage that had produced five sparkling children. We were well on our way.

So many people would affirm us in our lives. "You guys seem to be doing so great. God is blessing you all with success in business and a beautiful family."

While all of these things were true, and God had indeed blessed us with so much, Lacy and I felt a deeper stirring, a call to something more: a deeper commitment to our life with Jesus Christ, to know Him more, to love Him more, to serve Him more. And God used these two experiences to get my attention: a five-minute Francis Chan video on Facebook on a random Tuesday morning and a week-long mission trip to Mexico.

Two Rich Men Who Got It Wrong

We are all rich, whether we want to admit it or not, and it took me quite some time to accept that. Roughly half of the world's population lives on $5.50 per day, and over a quarter of the world's population lives on $3.20 per day.[2] You could probably take $3.20 per day out of my wallet every single day for the rest of my life, and not only would it not change the way I live, but I probably wouldn't even notice it.

Eleven percent of our world's population still lives with no access to clean water, and roughly one-fourth of the world lives daily with no improved sanitation (toilet and plumbing as we know it).[3] Think of that next time you sit on a toilet. Nearly two billion people in our world squat over a hole in the ground outside or in some type of shed covered in flies hovering over feces. Up to this point in my life, I had never considered myself rich, but looking back, I was a fool to think this way.

As time distanced me from our first mission trip, I began to reflect on so much, and I soon realized how spiritually mediocre I had become, how lukewarm. God was calling my family and me to something much deeper; he was calling us to leave a good and blessed life for a life far greater and even far more meaningful. All of this seemed to happen quite quickly, but looking back on it, we didn't make quick decisions. We sat back and sized things up for a while.

Two parables summed me up at this stage in my life. Both of them were Jesus encountering rich men, and sadly, both of them did not end well for the rich men. I'm sure you are familiar with both men. The first one can be found in Mark 10:17-31, when Jesus encounters the rich man who claims he had followed all the commandments since his youth but still wanted to know what he needed to do to inherit eternal life. Do you remember Jesus' response?

"You are lacking in one thing. Go, sell what you have, and give to the poor and you will have treasure in heaven; then come, follow me."

– Matthew 10: 20-21

And the rich man just can't do it. He can't part with his stuff for some reason. It's far too valuable to him, even more valuable than eternal life. That's a deep and dangerous attachment.

For years, as a cradle Catholic, I had heard about that encounter in the Gospels and thought, *stupid rich man, so selfish, how could he not part with all his stuff?* But now the tables were turning on me. I knew that if God was calling us to make disciples of all nations, I could not hold on to so many possessions and other passions. I would no longer be spending my days driving around town looking for lucrative real estate deals. My thoughts quickly turned into, *poor rich man, how could Jesus require that of him?* Or, *is Jesus asking him to give it all away?* I sensed Jesus asking me to give away some things and to walk away from some things, and that began to frighten me. We all know what happens to this man. He can't do it. The scriptures tell us that he walked away sad because he had many possessions.

I just couldn't imagine the thought of now being in this man's shoes and walking away from Jesus sadly because He had invited me into something so grand, but I wasn't willing to follow Him. Then in the scriptures, Jesus gives His infamous jab on wealth, whereby He states that it is easier for a camel to pass through the eye of a needle than for a rich man to enter the kingdom of heaven. Jesus' words, the truth, the Gospel, were coming at me, and they were coming at me fast.

The second encounter with a rich man was the man who had an incredible harvest, and his barns were no longer large enough to contain it all. You can find this story in Luke 12: 13-21. So he thought he would tear it all down and build bigger, larger ones, and then rest on his earnings and enjoy the good life. This is when Jesus piped up, spoiling his celebration, saying:

"You fool, this very night your life will be demanded of you; and the things you have prepared, to whom will they belong?"

– Luke 12:20

I had many of the same thoughts as this man in pursuit of my American Dream. In fact, I feel like this was me just a few years back. I had somewhat fallen into the mindset that to make money, to have success, meant you were blessed, and thus able to live a bigger and better life materially.

I was reading books about growing my wealth to create a bigger and better life for myself. Lacy and I were finally at a point where we were paying off all debts; we were saving money and acquiring great assets. In just a few years, some of them would be paid off, and we would have plenty of passive income. I had those years highlighted in my mind, *then* I would be able to fully serve God, and *then* I would be able to live life. Only once I had achieved more success. This was the plan.

But I also included Jesus in my plans. You see, I was going to make enough passive income by the time I was about forty-five to fifty years old to survive, and I planned to serve God more intently then. In my own way, I was this rich fool. I thought my plans were great, and perhaps they were; they certainly weren't bad.

I had just bought a bigger home and a better vehicle. But then, Jesus interrupted me abruptly. Among the poor in Mexico, He found me. Among those longing to be revived by the Holy Spirit, crammed into a small, rundown, Mexican chapel with no lights, He found me. He brought my heart back into focus with the poor, with His kingdom, with Himself. Once again, I had seen the face of Jesus in the poor, the hungry, the naked, the thirsty, and the lonely, and I had fallen in love with Him.

But when I sat alone to pray, I found how divided my heart was. I was in love with my possessions, and with my passions and dreams as well, and I didn't want to admit it. My barns were full, and my plans were set. Never in my life had I considered myself rich. Not for one minute, because there were always many people around who were far richer than me. I knew *those* people, and I encountered them every single day. I just needed to take a ride in my car to a nicer neighborhood. There were plenty of people richer than me.

What was I to do now? Jesus was calling me out, and at the same time was inviting me into a greater blessing He had prepared for me. I just couldn't see His plan in completion yet. I never can. He was calling me a rich man and challenging my well-thought-out plans and desires. He had a better plan for me and for my family, but did I trust Him?

Does any of this matter?

Lacy and I had felt the Holy Spirit urging and inviting us to move on from the life we had built. Eventually, we gave away or sold most of our stuff. It was a challenging process, but we erased our American Dream within about six months. That caused some pain and regret at first, yet it also gave us great joy and freedom in the end.

And so here we are now, all eight of us, somewhere out in the middle of Asia learning a new language and culture, eating strange foods, and walking around attracting stares, all in hopes of being Christ to the lost. For two years, we lived in rural Costa Rica, sleeping under bug nets, preaching the Gospel, and serving the poor, and it was the beginning of our glorious adventure. Terribly hot and sweaty, but oh so glorious.

Some people think we are crazy, like what type of an idiot does this? And some people marvel. But to our little family, it's just life, and it's just our new home. We are so far from perfect, and sometimes we feel like the most unqualified missionaries on earth, but we are merely striving to do what Jesus asks of us each day because, in the end, we long to be "rich in what matters to God" (Luke 12: 21).

I am slowly learning that to follow Jesus radically and sincerely means to hold on tighter to Him than to anything else that I want to hold on to. And that is so hard, and seemingly impossible at times, because I want to hold on to a lot of things. So often I still feel like that Rich Young Man, who just can't find a way to part with his earthly treasures and passions once God has asked him to do so.

Some people approach the end of their lives wondering if any of it mattered for anything other than their wellbeing and prosperity. And due to our broken nature, this type of existence is ingrained within us, and many of us are destined to that empty and shallow deathbed thinking: *did any of this matter?* I don't know about you, but I can't stand the thought of living my life in this way. How far this type of life is from the "abundant life" God offers to us through his Son, Jesus, in John 10:10. How far this type of life is from the original disciples of Jesus whose lives changed the entire world. I want and long for an abundance from God, and I want that same abundance lavished upon my wife, children, family, and every single person I meet.

I ran a marathon a few years ago and barely finished. I started strong and coasted for the first twenty miles, enjoying every breath and every drop of Sunday morning sweat. But the last six miles crushed me, physically and mentally.

I first found myself wondering, *can I even finish this race*, and then eventually, *does it even matter if I finish this race?*

That second question plagued me for what seemed like ten hours as I tried to complete the race. The question can still plague me today. The voices in my head had been defeating, and they had been crushing me.

I believe that many times in our lives, we ask ourselves that question in defeat: *Does any of this even matter?*

St. Paul tells us in 1 Corinthians 9:24-25 to "run the race to win because what is at stake is an imperishable crown." Meaning, this race of life on earth is for keeps. It's the only race we will get to run in that matters.

Eventually, I did finish that dang race, and as I ungracefully plowed across the finish line in great pain, I looked up and saw my beautiful wife and children glowing with smiles from ear to ear.

"Great job, Dad! You did it!"

Before crossing the line, I ran over to them and kissed them all. It was an exhilarating finish, and for a brief moment, all the pain in my knees, ankles, and legs were nonexistent. It was liberating.

This must be what entering heaven will be like, I thought, *but not quite . . .*

What will happen when you and I cross the finish line? Will our lives be worthy of applause? Will our spouses, children, and our God be there to say, "Great job! You did it, well done!"

Finally, a Rich Man Who Got it Right

I just want to treasure Jesus more than anything else in this life, and I want to live this life well for Christ in order to hear Him say, "Well done" (Matthew 25:21). For me, that has been a tall challenge. The world is filled with so many appealing sights, sounds, tastes, experiences, luxuries, and comforts, but in the end, none of them truly matter. Only Jesus matters. I long to be the third rich man who found his entire treasure in Jesus, but I'm just not there yet. You remember the man I am referring to, don't you? He is only mentioned ever so briefly and can be found in Matthew 13:44.

"The kingdom of heaven is like a treasure buried in a field, which a person finds and hides again, and out of joy goes and sells all that he has and buys that field."

– Matthew 13:44

Oh, how I long to be this man! To see Jesus as *the* treasure and to see everything else in my life as nothing and quickly fading in comparison to the goodness, glory, and treasure that is Christ. In my brokenness, I find it painfully hard to turn my back on the allures of *fools-treasure* that the world is constantly offering me. Fortunately, if nothing else, I feel like God redirecting our lives in this radical manner has allowed us to see Jesus more clearly, to see Him for the treasure He truly is as so many securities and familiarities have been stripped away from us. But again, we are still very far off.

So, have you found the field with the greatest treasure yet? What are you holding in your hands today that you need to scurry off and sell or give away? For me, it was much, and it continues to be much each day. What is consuming your days and nights? Because if we continue to hold on to these things, can we truly hold on to our only true and lasting treasure, Jesus Christ?

Chapter 2: Love Alone

"Without love, deeds, even the most brilliant, count as nothing."[4]

– St Therese of Lisieux

How in the world will I live with myself if she dies like this, I thought. Of course, Lacy's phone only had a 1 percent battery on it. It often does. But we picked it up anyway as it was our last and only hope. But once we realized what was happening, we simply begged out loud, "Come, Holy Spirit! Come, Holy Spirit!" I don't believe I have ever prayed that hard and sincerely in my entire life.

We were staying the night at our dear friends' Pablo and Yalile's home about two hours away and were up late with them, praying, eating, and visiting. They had become such great friends in a short but meaningful time, and they wanted us to come and spend some time with them in their home to discuss life as foreign missionaries. For so many years, they had served so faithfully in Costa Rica, but they felt God calling them even deeper in love and service. They wanted to become fulltime missionaries, and had so many questions.

When we headed back to our room, all of our kids were sound asleep except Lily, who was two at the time. Lacy and I brushed our teeth, and I walked out of the bathroom to enter the bedroom only to find the brightest and most colorful snake I had ever seen. Snakes and sharks are by far my biggest fears. This snake was so bright I actually thought and yelled out loud to Lacy, "I hope that thing is fake!"

Its bright yellows and reds looked like wet paint. But then I saw the movement in its slithery skin, and my jaw dropped. It was a coral snake, and it was sprawled out upon my suitcase facing Lily, Lacy, and I, roughly two feet away from us. I didn't know what to do, so I quietly closed the door hoping it wouldn't be startled and move. All the rest of the kids were in that room, but they were a good ten yards away from him. Or so I thought. Welcome to every parent's worst nightmare.

Thank God for that 1 percent. We called, and instantly, Pablo and his son came rushing in with machetes and shovels. I swear Costa Ricans eat, sleep, and dream with machetes in their hands. Everything was happening so fast that I could not remember if it was a poisonous coral or not. The poisonous coral snake is red touching yellow with black also mixed in, thus the saying r*ed and yellow kills a fellow*. I figured we would find out in a moment based on their noise level upon entering into the room.

The screaming was through the roof! They had made their entrance into the room. Indeed a poisonous coral snake. The two of them realized what Lacy and I did not see; the snake was lying just twelve inches away from my sweet five-year-old daughter Miriam's face. I had no clue that she was lying in bed next to the bathroom; I completely didn't see her there when we walked into the room.

They needed to get the snake out of her face without alarming it too much, causing it to attack. Behind that closed bathroom door seemed an eternity, and all Lacy and I could do was pray. Pray and hope that our prayers mattered for *something*, hope that our prayers mattered to *someone.*

We heard the two of them screaming out Spanish commands to one another. It got really loud. I was freaking out. I was legitimately wondering how stupid I was for moving away from the United States of America at this point.

What are we doing here? What have I done? How in the world will I live with myself if Miriam gets bit and dies like this? And we waited.

Eventually, loud Spanish rejoicing broke out, and I figured we were in the clear. They had indeed escorted the snake outside somehow and cut his head off. My sweet Miriam slept like a beautiful angel the entire time and never woke up. In fact, none of our five kids in there ever woke up during the entire crazy ordeal. Crazy how a squeaky door at home wakes every last one of them, but somehow, on this particular night, a full-blown bloody battle with two men, sharp machetes, and a coral snake didn't cause a single one of them to budge.

God's Enormous, Loving Hands

I can't wait to be in Heaven one day and ask God to replay that crazy scene. I want to count the saints and angels around my sweet Miriam. I want to see how large the palm of God's hand was as He held Miriam in it, protecting her from a potentially deadly attack. God's love for us is so enormous yet so intimate, intimate enough to hold us in the palm of His hand. Intimate enough for me to cry out to Him as the Psalmist does in Psalm 139:7:

> *"Though I walk in the midst of dangers, you guard my life when my enemies rage. You stretch out your hand; your right hand saves me."*

I often wonder how most of the world would respond if we encountered this type of intimate love and protection our God offers us, to see and feel the callouses and the pulse on the hands of God our Father. To know and understand that He is always that close to us. Would there be so much suffering, pain, and brokenness? Would there be so much unbelief and anger directed toward an all-loving God? But I fear that many of us alive today usually feel as though we are journeying through life alone, with no one guiding us, and no one loving us.

It seems that every day, I am walking by and encountering individuals who are deeply desperate to be held by God in the manner my sweet Miriam was held that night. I see them everywhere, empty-eyed and heavily burdened. Perhaps you do, too? I wish I could find a way to cut through all the nonsense and strip away all that they experienced or "knew" about God that was negative, all that kept them from God. I wish I could strip away every horrible encounter they had with a Christian and every horrendous decision they ever made. And at that moment, I wish I could airdrop them into the hands of our all-knowing and all-loving God. I think the world would be a greater place, a more loving place, and I think all of us would see God for who He is, because:

"Beloved, let us love one another, because love is of God; everyone who loves is begotten by God and knows God. Whoever is without love does not know God, for God is love."

– 1 John 4: 7-8

Our family has literally traveled around the world, stopping or living in just under ten countries, and God willing we are just getting started. Among the world's thousands of languages, I have realized that only love is the universal language. There is no translation needed, and there is no denying it when you see it. Love is enough to bridge a gap of hatred between countries, and love is enough to connect people from opposite sides of the world. Love is worth losing everything for. Yes, we have stomped upon and killed many snakes along the way. In fact, since the coral snake incident, our family has had three other crazy and close encounters with snakes. The snakes are everywhere, seeking to destroy all of us, but in the end, only love remains for it is the greatest of all (1 Corinthians 13:13).

I'm thirsty; I'm thirsty!

Just yesterday, our family had the challenge, yet honor, of witnessing one of our friends, Joseph, on his death bed. He was in Ward C-5 at a large and rundown public hospital in Asia. The place was old and filled to capacity, thus making him one of about one hundred people in that ward withering away together. He was in a brutal battle with the final stages of the AIDS virus, an illness which knows no limits and has no mercy.

Once a bright-eyed and sharp professor with the world before him and a great audience listening to him, he was now withering away in his thirties. Alone. He looked one hundred years old.

He clung to a dingy bed sheet with his frail fingers, and his shaky voice cried out to us, "I'm thirsty! I'm thirsty!" His lips were parched, and he was desperate. He couldn't stop crying out these words, and I knew the thirst he had was a deep, spiritual one, one we have all tasted before. After giving him water to drink, we laid our hands upon him in prayer. I couldn't help but recall the words of Jesus with the Samaritan woman at the well.

"Everyone who drinks this water will be thirsty again, but whoever drinks the water I shall give will never thirst; the water I shall give will become in him a spring of water welling up to eternal life."

– John 4: 13-14

I walked away from his bed and spoke with his nurse, who, in a sobering voice, informed me that his time was coming; death was now imminent. She had watched him slowly break down over the last few days, and all his vital organs were now failing.

I returned to his bedside with one of my daughters and grabbed his hand and prayed with him one last time. I teared up thinking how his entire family had abandoned him, and now he was dying alone in this stale hospital bed. Sadly, we were the only ones who had come to visit him in his three-week stay at the hospital. Holding his feeble hand, I begged God for a down poor of the living water of his mercy and forgiveness to be poured out upon my friend. I begged God to take away my friend's pain and suffering and welcome him into the restful shores of eternity. The next morning, Joseph died in his bed alone.

I feel like God has given me the opportunity to drink deeply of his waters of eternal life. Sometimes, I feel it boiling over within me. I want to give it away; I long to give it away. I have come to realize that there are millions, and even billions, of people like my friend Joseph, alone and dying in their own brokenness, pains, illness, and sin. There are so many Samaritans dying of thirst at the well, many of them seeking a water that does not last. There is so much to be done and so much love to be given. I can't sit on the sidelines anymore.

Chapter 3: The Judgment of the Nations

"It would be considered theft on our part if we did not give to someone in greater need than we are."

– St Francis of Assisi

As we approached the beaten up and worn down, dilapidated house, we could see the sun pouring right into it. The place was falling, no glass on the windows, rotten second or third-hand boards somehow fastened to the dirt floor. The house was positioned at the very bottom of a hill, wedging it between a natural drainage laguna and the waste site of a wood mill. We were greeted by wandering cats, flies, and the stench of urine, but more seared into our hearts and memories were the enormous, life-giving smiles we were greeted with that day.

Rosario is in her sixties, and a stroke has left her nearly paralyzed from the waist down. She can't walk, and the old wheelchair she has is nearly useless on her dirt floor. She can hardly speak either, another casualty of her stroke. But she can smile. Boy, can she smile. She has this incredible smile that spontaneously breaks into laughter when she sees us. It lifts our spirits like a rocket blast. She's always smiling. Well, to be honest, she's usually smiling when she sees one of my children. She loves children.

When we met her, she had no plumbing in her home save for an outhouse up the hill behind her home, which she clearly could not make it to. So she uses the bathroom in a bedpan underneath a hole carved into a wooden bench which she perches upon all day, every day. She often smells of urine and constantly has flies swarming around her. But her contagious smile outshines her surroundings. She is so beautiful. Glorious.

Her husband, Felipe, is a piece of work. He is quick-witted, sharp, and short, like five-foot-two or so. He migrated from Nicaragua into Costa Rica during the civil war in Nicaragua in the 1980s. He is the type of person whose presence is so accommodating he could befriend and disarm the most hardened of hearts. He is all smiles, too.

He is eighty-four years old and journeyed over a month on foot years ago to flee the oppression in his country. He often tells us stories of the brutalities of walking through the jungles of southern Nicaragua and into northern Costa Rica in an attempt to discover a better life: barefoot in the scorching hot mountains, wild animals, turbulent and tropical rainy seasons, hardly finding food to eat. It sounds horrible. His first wife died back home in Nicaragua during this time, and he never saw her again, and somehow, he ended up here in Northern Costa Rica, living what he calls "a better life."

For some reason, he and I immediately just hit it off. He speaks choppy English at times, and my Spanish is, of course, choppy as well. I love this man with all my heart. Both of my grandfathers have passed away, so I instantly came to view him as a grandfather. He is a beautiful and special soul. I can honestly tell you that these two people quickly became my favorite two people here in Costa Rica. They are a true thing of beauty.

I need to cut to the chase, though. Felipe and Rosario have absolutely nothing. They were probably born into nothing, and they will always have absolutely nothing. And they will die with absolutely nothing. Their home is a small, three-hundred-square-foot wood frame on a dirt floor. No lights, an old well for water, a wood-burning stove, and no bathroom. I grew up in Louisiana, and I can't say I have ever seen a barn down south for horses in such bad condition. They have nothing, yet they are richer than me.

Jesus has so much to say regarding the poor and has a deep love and even preference for them. He tells us that the good news *must* be preached to them (Luke 7:22-23). But the poor often fail to get my attention unless I am truly confronted with them. And in most cases, I have lived my life far removed from them, my neighborhood over here and theirs over there. Sure I may have a superficial or even childlike sympathy when I encounter them, but many times, I am not like Jesus, who seems to place them first on His list of importance.

It's almost as if Jesus knew how much we would avoid and marginalize the poor, so He seems to just lay it all out on the line for us regarding the poor in Matthew 25:31-46. The passage is a bit long, but it is worth every word to reread:

> *When the Son of Man comes in his glory, and all the angels with him, he will sit upon his glorious throne, and all the nations will be assembled before him. And he will separate them one from another, as a shepherd separates a sheep from the goats. He will place the sheep on his right and the goats on his left. Then the king will say to those on his right, "Come, you who are blessed by my father. Inherit the kingdom prepared for you from the foundation of the world. For I was hungry and you gave me food, I was thirsty and you gave me drink, a stranger and you welcomed me, naked and you clothed me, ill and you cared for me, in prison and you visited me." Then the righteous will answer him and say, "Lord, when did we see you hungry and feed you, or thirsty and give you drink? When did we see you a stranger and welcome you, or naked and clothe you? When did we see you ill or in prison and visit you?" And the king will say to them in reply, "Amen, I say to you,*

> *whatever you did for one of these least brothers of mine, you did for me." Then he will say to those on his left, "Depart from me, you accursed, into the eternal fire prepared for the devil and his angels. For I was hungry and you gave me no food, I was thirsty and you gave me no drink, a stranger and you gave me no welcome, naked and you gave me no clothing, ill and in prison, and you did not care for me." Then they will answer and say, "Lord, when did we see you hungry or thirsty or a stranger or naked or ill or in prison, and not minister to your needs?" He will answer them, "Amen, I say to you, what you did not do for one of these least ones, you did not do for me." And these will go off to eternal punishment, but the righteous to eternal life.*

As I read this passage, I am deeply challenged, and my takeaway is simple and twofold: First, I must seek, love, and serve the poor, or there will be grave and eternal consequences. And second, in serving the poor, I will inherit eternal life while falling deeper in love with Jesus, because He is the poor.

Catholic author and speaker Chris Stefanick says, "In Matthew 25, it's as if Jesus gives us all the answers to the final exam before giving us the test."[5] But Jesus is clear with us, there will be a test or judgment, and how we love those in the margins will be how we are judged. Look around you. Who are the poor, hungry, thirsty, ill, imprisoned, naked, and left behind? Perhaps they don't live in your neighborhood. Perhaps they do. Are we serving their needs at all? For me, this is tough, and I have signed up to be a world missionary dedicated to serving the poor and preaching the Gospel to them.

But I must admit it was even tougher for me living in America. It was tougher for me because, in America, I could easily just live as if the poor did not exist. I could separate myself from them easier. My neighborhood, for the most part, was not accessible to the poor. They didn't live there. I did not generally encounter them at my office or the other businesses I frequented weekly. And the poor generally didn't run around in my social circles. So unless I was going to seek them out, which now and then I did, I really wouldn't bump into them.

Jesus doesn't want us to just accidentally bump into a poor person by chance one day; He wants us to have sincere and real loving relationships with them. Them and us. Us and them. Coming to know, love, and understand one another living in the same community. Think about what He is saying to us in Matthew 25. He *is* the hungry, thirsty, stranger, ill, and imprisoned. So why would I not run out to meet Him? This is Jesus before me. Perhaps it's so challenging because it's so inconvenient?

Daniel's Dignity

Not long after we moved into Coopevega, Costa Rica, I encountered the local pack of drunk men who were always wandering the streets. Daniel seemed to be the ring leader. He was a well-known *borracho* (drunk) in our small town. At times, he's a mess, but he has so many natural gifts and even possesses tremendous charm. "Don't help him; we have all been burned by Daniel!," they would warn me as they saw me speaking with him.

Daniel's story was no different than most people with a drinking or drug problem. He had burned every bridge and opportunity he had. His family wouldn't let him back inside their home because he was always drunk or high. He couldn't keep steady employment because employment is sparse there, and he is often drinking. But when he is sober, he is a different guy. His thoughts are lucid, and his heart is huge. He used to work in tourism along Costa Rica's coast, so he has some great social skills and can speak some English and French.

When we met, we seemed to hit it off. He always seemed to find me and always seemed to be hungry. So we started to feed him. He would just come over hungry, almost always after he drank his earnings away and had slept in the graveyard or a mountain for the night. He had no home, car, or anything. He had this book sack he would carry around with him, and that's all. He wore the crosses we gave him, my old t-shirts, and a nice pair of Nikes he somehow convinced me to give him.

Daniel was always speaking of his desire to kick his addiction. At this stage of his life, it was manifested most in alcohol. He knew it was a real demon, and he longed to be freed from it. Often I cringed when he came over because it was the same thing over and over again. "Give me some food, please. I'm drunk again. I have no place to live. Please pray with me to change." But this was Jesus. Daniel was Jesus at my doorstep; I just had to have the eyes to see Him.

I don't know about you, but I am tired of hearing from people other than Jesus about how I should treat people like Daniel.

"Don't give him anything; he doesn't deserve it."

"It's best that you don't feed him, or else he will keep coming back into our neighborhood."

Or, "You have better and more important things to do than talk to drunk men."

Jesus never said these things about the poor in scripture. I think, in our imaginations, we believe that the poor Jesus is referring to are these perfect, unfortunate humans who, by some horrible twist of fate, have become poor. But they happen to be as sweet and tender as our grandmother and as sanitized as a newborn baby in a hospital. That's rarely the case. The poor are dirty, they often stink, and they are most times more than inconvenient. If we reach out to the poor, they will drain us of our time, they will take advantage of our talents, and they will convince us to spend our money on them. And that's okay. How else are we to embrace them as Jesus is calling us to do?

I also believe I need to change my approach to how I treat the poor. Sure, it is good and holy to want to better their situation in life, but sometimes, all Jesus is asking me to do is to serve them at that moment. I have found that rarely am I called to "fix" their lives. God can do that. The vast majority of the time, I am not being called to change their economic wellbeing or their financial status. I am just called to love them, and loving them often means simply responding to their most immediate needs. Is this not the heart of Matthew 25? Feed me, clothe me, visit me. How hard can that be? But too often I ask, *well, does he need this food or clothes, or is he taking advantage of me?* Who cares! Jesus just asks for me to do these things, not necessarily to fully understand them. But I have to be convinced that Jesus is in the poor, and that is hard. I challenge myself to reread Matthew 25 often because now that I am away from my nice neighborhood in America, the poor are all around, and they are always asking for something.

One day, when Daniel had been sober and reading his Bible for about a month, he expressed to me how badly he wanted to sleep inside a house, to get inside away from the elements and horrible mosquitoes. He had been working hard and wanted to find a place to rent, and he wanted to know if I would help him find a place. “For sure, Daniel! Anything for my brother.” Lacy and I even thought we would pay his first month’s rent.

We lived in an extremely small town, so our options were very limited, especially since he had burned just about every landlord in town. As we drove around looking for a house, our plan was for him to stay in my van, and I would get out and ask each landlord if I could rent the place. I emphasized to Daniel how important it was for him to remain in the van at least while I got the conversation going. One by one, each landlord seemed eager to rent to *me*.

"Yes, the house is available, Felipe, but how will your entire family fit into this small house?" And that's when I would bring up my man Daniel.

"Well, you see, I am renting the place for a dear friend of mine," I would say.

"Oh, that's so kind of you," they would say.

To which I would respond, "Well, let me go and get him. He's in the van." And out would pop Daniel with a smile like he was in some game show behind a curtain.

Turns out, our plan was a bit short-sighted as one by one each landlord turned us down. Daniel chuckled at our first denial, explaining to the lady how he had been sober for almost a month and that he had been reading his Bible and wanted to change. He frowned at our next denial and then was in tears by the third one. Real, grown-man tears.

He knew he had wasted his life and burned bridges; you could see it in his eyes. He knew people in town were afraid of him, but his heart still hurt. We were both determined, and eventually, I convinced a sweet lady with a very reasonable doubt in her eyes to let us rent for him. She warned me how this would end, and I assured her that I agreed it would probably end with my paying his last month's rent and repairing some damages he would make along the way. I simply begged her to take a chance on Daniel because he was worth it. Even if this was his fifteenth chance, he was still worth it, right?

I think sometimes I view the poor and needy as people who are only warranted one chance, but I would give myself or someone with the financial means to advance me fifteen chances in one day. If Jesus is truly the poor person at my feet, then I must give them all the chances He asks me to give them. I have to live and love the poor like my chance with them is the only one they have.

"I was hungry and you gave me food, I was thirsty and you gave me drink, a stranger and you welcomed me, naked and you clothed me, ill and you cared for me, in prison and you visited me."

– Matthew 25:35-36

We did it big for Daniel's move in. He was so proud when his landlord handed over the keys to him. He gave me a copy and told me this was *our* place. I almost teared up at his excitement and hospitality. I thought for about thirty seconds how insane it would have been to live with Daniel, even for just a week, but declined his offer, telling him that this was his place and he was to be responsible and care for the place like it was his own. Plus, my wife expected me to live with her.

We took a picture with him holding the keys to his new place that I will forever cherish in my memory. Behind his second or third-hand Hooters t-shirt and my Nike shoes was an enormous smile and sense of pride that I will always remember. It was life-changing for me. Glorious. He had been given an opportunity. He had been treated like a human being, with dignity. It was a thing of beauty. All his friends were stoked that he finally had his place, and he told them that no one was to drink in his home and that it would be a sacred place. He came over to my house the next day and asked if we could start an AA meeting in his ("our" as he kept referring to it) new living room. He said we could read the Bible and pray with one another and all his *borracho* friends for strength to overcome their disease. I was floored and humbled.

The next night, we met, and there were close to twenty people there. I cooked a meal, and Daniel welcomed everyone in. It may have been the most unorthodox AA meeting of all time, but on that night, I knew we were sitting in the center of God's will. We were in his kingdom, building it. We prayed over one another, we ate, and read the Bible. Real men shed real-man tears as they confessed how far they had fallen from grace but how much they longed to change. The poor and unwanted of this small town gathered around one another and cared for one another. It was a beautiful evening I will never forget.

I felt like, for that one night, God had moved so many mountains in the lives of these men, and they were noticing it. They were no longer homeless and marginalized in that small town where their faults were constantly on display before everyone. They reclaimed their dignity and authenticity. You could see their individual personalities all coming out. Each man had unique gifts and a unique story to tell. I could no longer lump them together as "the pack of drunk men outside the store." Behind their constant ask for money, I could now see their smiles, their hopes, and even some of their dreams. I could see Christ and finally had the opportunity to let them know that.

Our Exam

It seems like nothing excites Felipe and Rosario more than a visit from our family. I believe this to be true because they are always so excited when we walk through their doorway. I feel like a million bucks every time. Sometimes we bring food with us for them, and sometimes we do not, but I am always so humbled to realize that more than food, or clothes, or money, they always just seem to long for our presence. They long for love. Don't we all?

"Thank you for coming. No one ever comes to visit us but your family and the other missionaries. Everyone just views us as poor people who don't fit in and who have nothing to offer. Thank you so much." They tell us this so often, and it breaks my heart and builds it back up in the same sentence.

They teach me so much about where I can find Jesus. He is always just sitting there waiting inside the hearts and needs of the poor, the forgotten, and marginalized. When I leave their home, I am transformed because I have had an undeniable encounter with Jesus Christ.

And so how will our exam go? The answers have indeed been given to us, and the test is being played out right now. A world of people in need, and you and I are a part of the richest nation in the history of the world. We have to stop living lives of greed and self-interest and begin pursuing the needs of the poor if we are to become more like Jesus. Our hearts must burn with a passion for them, and their interests and desires must become our own. Sure it's challenging, and we will have to let go of some of our desires and plans to accommodate the poor, but in the end, it is indeed Jesus Christ Himself that we are serving.

Have you ever experienced something so amazing, so glorious that you immediately wish you could share it with the world? I wish every person alive could have been sitting around that circle in Daniel's house that night. Broken men had the chance to reclaim their God-given dignity and start over again.

Chapter 4: The Greatest Commission

"The Great Commission is not an option to be considered; it is a command to be obeyed."

– Hudson Taylor

While living in America, sometimes our family would bring single moms and their children with us to Church on Sunday mornings. These were usually young women we had met at a local crisis pregnancy center who at one point pondered having an abortion, but because of the grace of God and their courage to trust in Him, they had their babies. Many of these women were coming off drugs and still cleaning up their lives. They were rough around the edges, sometimes a bit dangerous, and didn't always fit into our affluent parish.

Among them was a sweet girl named Mary. I can specifically remember her walking up the communion line with us one Sunday morning. While our large and loud family usually can attract some stares on our own, on this day, my heart broke for Mary as all eyes seemed glued to her walking down that long aisle. It was so clear that this poor, young girl wasn't "one of us." Her teeth were crooked and rotting, and her hair was quite unkempt. On the exterior, she looked nothing like anyone in that Church. But on the inside, she was exactly, exactly, the same as all of us, created by God in His divine image, yet broken from the heaviness of life. She was like a big, blue, sore thumb on a perfectly manicured hand.

At that point, I wished we had all dressed down quite a bit to match her worn out and dingy clothing. Yet she walked down the aisle so faithfully and received a blessing from the priest. She desired Jesus so much, she was so honored to be there with us all,

Bible in hand, her heart now set on things above, walking in a new direction.

I don't blame the people in my Church for staring at her. I would have been staring as well if I weren't right next to her. In line. I think I was just embarrassed that as a whole, our Church was so surprised to see someone like her among us, in Church seeking God. At that moment, I realized that I needed to do better in terms of inviting people into the life of Christ, inviting them into the life of the Church; that way she wouldn't be the only one who stood out there. After all, I think she may have been the first person I had brought with me to Church in a long time.

It appeared that she was the only "outsider" like herself invited that morning. My heart hurt for her and for the many like her in my community that had yet to receive an invitation to church. There should be an entire section just like her there in attendance every Sunday, except completely integrated into the body of the Church. Shouldn't our churches be filled with people like her? People who look like they have lost their way and people who look like someone just found them among some of their toughest days and invited them off the streets and into the Church of Jesus Christ? Christ established His Church for her and for people with deep pains like her; who am I to not welcome her in?

After Mass, I wanted to say to her, "I'm so sorry you didn't fit into my Church, and I'm so sorry there was no one like you there this morning. We sort of stink at inviting new people in, but I promise you we will do better. This Church is for you. In fact, Jesus set this Church up precisely for people like you."

I am deeply challenged by the words of Pope Francis in *Joy of the Gospel* when he states, "The salvation which God has wrought, and the Church joyfully proclaims, is for everyone. God has found a way to unite Himself to every human being in every age."[6] And again, "Jesus did not tell the apostles to form an exclusive and elite group."[7]

Jesus did not establish a social club for us, the elite, but sometimes when I glance around the Church, it seems that way. It seems like perhaps we just gather with one another and forget about those like Mary, those who perhaps need Jesus the most, those living in the worst and most painful chapters of their lives.

If I am to take the Great Commission seriously, then I have to constantly find myself among those who are most in need. I have to remove myself from the elite and exclusive and bring the Good News to the lost. It is my job to go outside of the Church and proclaim the Good News, not simply remain inside the Church walls feeding myself. I have to ask myself, *who am I bringing into the life of the Church? Who am I inviting into this good news?* Because, if I just keep the love of God to myself, then I believe I am completely missing the entire essence of what it means to proclaim Christ as Lord and Savior.

If my life is only surrounded by those who believe in Jesus and keep all of His commands, then I have to reflect upon the life of Jesus and recall that He found Himself among the unclean and lost, among those who needed Him most. I have to remember Jesus' encounter with the Scribes and Pharisees as He was sitting with tax collectors and sinners. The Scribes and Pharisees questioned why He would do such a thing, spend His time with these unclean people. To which He boldly replied, "Those who are well do not need a physician, but the sick do. I did not come to call the righteous but sinners" (Mark 2:17). Am I anything like Jesus?

No Greater Mission

The mission of the Church is to evangelize. While that is a simple statement to write down on paper, it is a challenging mission to undertake personally. Our family has traveled around the world, and we have encountered the same issue in all parts of the world. As a whole, we as a Church aren't taking the Great Commission very seriously. And that starts with me. The Great Commission is Great because it is given to us from Jesus Christ Himself, and it portrays and presents the greatest love story ever known to man, and this story has and will forever change lives. But it is not easy. Further, it is the greatest challenge known to man.

The two most direct commands of Jesus Christ to His disciples to go and make disciples of all nations can be found in the following verses:

"All power in heaven and earth has been given to me. Go, therefore, and make disciples of all nations, baptizing them in the name of the Father, and of the Son, and of the Holy Spirit, teaching them to observe all that I have commanded you."

– Matthew 28:17-20

"Go into the whole world and proclaim the Gospel to every creature. Whoever believes and is baptized will be saved; whoever does not believe will be condemned."

– Mark 16:15-16

These disciples of Jesus Christ received these words with great faith, and after receiving the power and comfort of the Holy Spirit, they went out and proclaimed the Good News to the entire world as they knew it. The name and renown of the Lord Jesus and the Church grew as a result of their faith. All of them, except for John, died a martyr's death, receiving the grand prize of all discipleship.

This is the mission of the Church. Everything we think, do, or pray as Catholics springs forth from this command of Jesus, and everything points us back to this command. Because of this command, our faith is not our own, and our faith cannot be hidden. It must flow out of us with great humility and courage.

Sometimes we can make it so complicated, trying to proclaim the Good News, but if we look at the words of Jesus, He breaks it down for us, thus simplifying how it can look in our lives.

Go

To *go* means that I have to be willing to leave my own comforts and plans behind. I often think back to the earliest disciples of Jesus. Can you imagine being the heir apparent to your family business and hearing Jesus call your name to *immediately* leave it all behind? And then to do so like James and John did, thus leaving your father untangling the nets of the family business, wondering why in the world you would leave it all behind to follow this radical man, Jesus (Matthew 4: 21-22)? To go implies that I am leaving something or somewhere to bring the Gospel to someone. What is it that I am leaving to share the Gospel?

The aspect of *going* is the entire hinge of the Great Commission, and it is the reason that as a Church, we struggle so much with the Great Commission of Christ. We rarely are willing to *go* or to let go of what we have going on in our lives. I have found that in my own life it is easier and more convenient to understand the Great Commission as "*stay* and make disciples of my *own* nation within my own comforts and on my own timeline," rather than" *go* and make disciples of *all* nations." And therein is the entire challenge of the Great Commission. As a whole, we are not willing to *go*, even if it just means *going* to the other side of town where perhaps there is more need.

Make Disciples of All Nations

Making disciples is, in my opinion, the most challenging and most forgotten aspect of the Great Commission. The first challenge is that for me to make a disciple, I have to actually be a disciple of Jesus Christ. I have to have sat at the feet of the master for extended periods of time, just listening to His voice and pondering all that He is. Then, I have to follow Him and walk with Him so as to know the steps He has taken and is still taking in the world today. My life has to be so extremely saturated with the Word of God and the sacraments that my actions spring forth from it. I have to put Christ in all things. Then, and only then, can I attempt to make a disciple.

Making disciples requires me to allow someone to sit at my feet for a long period of time seeing the great love I have for Jesus Christ. I have to be willing to invite them into my life and see the good, bad, and ugly, yet still understand that Jesus is Lord over all of these aspects of my life. I have to be willing to invite them deeply into the life of Christ, including a sacramental life, a life rooted in the scriptures and a life dedicated to the service of God and others. A dear mentor once told me to keep it simple and seek out three to five people each year to disciple. I think of the life of Jesus. He preached and taught to great crowds, but He discipled very few, namely His twelve. I believe this is the greatest example for us.

Making disciples is not glamorous, and it takes our precious time. If I am willing to make a disciple, then I am willing to create precious time for someone and take them into who I am, thus showing them Christ on a much deeper level. After a few years, this person has garnered that which is most precious to me, my love for Jesus Christ. This type of knowledge and understanding cannot occur overnight. On top of that, I am called by Jesus to consider making disciples of *all nations* and not just my own. This is a tall challenge, one that will stretch my comforts and security. We can look at what *all nations* means more in depth in a later chapter.

Baptize

I sense that as a Church, by and large, we do this part of the Great Commission the easiest. Those who come to us to be baptized, whether it be a parent with their infant or an adult, can be guided through a very clear and concise program to provide them with the sacrament of baptism. I sense the great challenge in me, and the life of the Church is presenting and inviting those outside the Church into a sacramental life— to those way out on the fringes. I believe this is where our challenge as a Church lies. It's easy for us to baptize those who come to us all cleaned up and ready to go, but who have I gone out and pursued and invited, others apart from Christ, into baptism? While we lived in Costa Rica, baptism was such a monumental event, because where we lived, families didn't just automatically show up to have their children baptized immediately after birth. Many of their parents didn't attend Church or were somewhat lapsed in their faith. Godparents were tough to find, and in some cases, impossible to find, in these small pueblos because so few people were living out their faith authentically.

Teach

To teach someone all that Christ has commanded us is a tall task as well, but again, Christ has given us a clear guidepost through the teachings of the Word of God and the teachings of the Church. Much like discipleship, this aspect of the Great Commission takes time and cannot be performed overnight. But like all of the other aspects of the Great Commission, it hinges on my willingness to go. If I never go and engage someone, then I can never teach them. The Church contains a wellspring of life-giving teachings and documents. Many so rich in grace that, once people begin to read into them, their lives are transformed. One temptation I see in our Church is to assume that teaching people about Christ and the Church is the end goal. While catechesis is important, without proper and life-giving discipleship, it can empty and lifeless.

Living with Intention

While we are now removed from many of the former distractions of our lives, we still have many things that keep us from spreading the Good News of Jesus Christ. I find that one way to take the Great Commission seriously is to treat it like the command that it is. From birth, I have been drilled and drilled to keep the Ten Commandments. When I stumble and choose to sin, I express sorrow to God, repent, and run to the sacrament of Confession. I have to view the Great Commission as the Eleventh Commandment, or perhaps the second one at least. This command of Jesus is just that, a command—not a suggestion.

I imagine it would have been easy for the apostles of Christ to receive the Great Commission like I often do, as a mere suggestion. What would the Church look like today? Would the name of Christ be known among any of us at all if they did so? Like the apostles, I have to make Jesus and His Great Commission my priority. It has to be the driving force of my life. I can't put it on the back burner and forget about it; it must remain in the front of my heart and mind.

Like anything else important in my life, I must learn to prioritize it, or making disciples among all nations simply won't be a part of my life. I have found that constantly asking the following questions to myself can be of great assistance:

1. Who is the Holy Spirit sending me to today?

2. What three to five people has the Holy Spirit placed into my life that I can disciple? Am I reaching out to them and meeting with them at least monthly?
3. Who am I inviting into baptism (or other sacraments) and a deeper life of grace within the Church?
4. Who am I teaching about the commands and desires of Christ? (Many times, the answer to this question is the same answer to the second question.)
5. Can I think of anyone who would state that they have been discipled by me?

The Great Commission is For All

Basri's room is the first one on the right as we walk into the Aids Home. He is roommates with three other men who are all bedridden or wheelchair-bound. One of his roommates was Joseph, who you remember passed away last week in the hospital, crying out how thirsty he was.

Basri is bedridden as well and has been for about six years. Barring a miracle, he will continue to be bound to that bed until he dies. He was born a male, but at some stage in life decided to identify as a female. For over forty years, he was a trans-prostitute who ran a small brothel in Southeast Asia. At some point along in this deceiving and risky lifestyle, he contracted HIV, which has now developed into the last stages of the AIDS virus. The AIDS virus is intense and has sympathy for no one. Now, he is confined to a small hospital bed as his body and what remains of his life simply wither away in his small room.

He had a stroke that has coiled his arms and legs up pretty severely and prevents him from speaking clearly; his skin clings to his frail and brittle bones. This disease has eroded everything he has: mind, spirit, and body. It’s sad to witness.

We walk in to visit him every Friday, and he greets us with a great but struggling smile. It's really all he can muster up. He loves holding Andrew's small hand, he loves our girls reading to him, and I imagine he longs for a day when he can abandon his world of pain and suffering. He tries to speak to us, but we can rarely understand much of what he has to say.

The saddest part about Basri's life is that he is a Muslim man born into a Muslim country, which forbids him from accepting Jesus into his life in any capacity. He is nearly unable to speak, so many days, I just sit with him and show him a small picture of Jesus while I pray for him. I have such a deep longing within me to let him know how madly in love Jesus is with him and that Jesus is the one who sent our crazy family to spend Fridays with him. Jesus loves him, and only Jesus can forgive him and reconcile him to God, his Father.

There are so many people like Basri in this enormous world. So many men, women, and children who have lost their way and are now living in despair, regret, and pain. Some, like Basri, live with horrible physical pain, and some without. Some live in Muslim countries and some in Christian countries. Each Friday, I sit with Basri in prayer, seeking ways to share the love and truth of Jesus Christ with him. Jesus has been so clear with us that we are to Go and find the Basris of this world, proclaiming the Gospel to them. You or I may most likely be their only encounter with Jesus Christ. As a baptized Christian missionary disciple of Jesus Christ, it is my responsibility to run out and find these people, and introduce them to the deep love of Jesus.

Look around you and see who is most in need. Usually, it will not be the person sitting next to you in Church. While those in our pews have deep and meaningful needs, I have to understand that there are so many millions and even billions of people in this world who are not sitting in Church each week hearing the Word of God proclaimed; there are billions who have never heard of our Jesus.

"Go rather to the lost sheep of the house of Israel. As you go, make this proclamation: The Kingdom of God is at hand. Cure the sick, raise the dead, cleanse lepers, drive out demons. Without cost you have received; without cost you are to give."

– Matthew 10: 6-7

Chapter 5: Show Me Your Treasure

"It is Jesus that you seek when you dream of happiness; He is waiting for you when nothing else you find satisfies you."[8]

– Pope Saint John Paul II

I remember the first big real estate deal I ever did. I was in way over my skis. A friend of mine and I had stumbled upon this amazing investment opportunity. It was a home run, an easy deal, and the man who owned it really wanted to sell it to me. I clearly couldn't afford it on my own, but I already knew who my partner would be. He was a trusted friend and a man of great integrity who was always in my ear asking me to bring him a great deal. I made one call, and it was done. He had a few other buddies who would all partner up with us, and I would run the day to day management of it while they put up the bulk of the cash. All of these partners were so well put together financially. Most of them were tried and truly successful in oil and gas. I, on the other hand, was younger and trying to make my way in real estate.

I'll never forget presenting my personal financial statement to the bank in an effort to obtain financing. It must have been like a great game of "one of these does not look like the others." For those of you who may not be familiar with a personal financial statement, it is simply two lists of everything you own and everything you owe with a given monetary amount for each item. The idea is obviously to own more than you owe, and the difference between the two is your "personal net worth." Banks use it to analyze who they are lending money to, and businessmen and businesswomen often pride their existence upon it. These guys were all worth multi-millions and aiming at a billion, and I was basically a break-even at best financially on paper.

I must admit, from that point on in my career in real estate, I became very obsessed with my personal financial statement. I updated it often, and I kept it on my desk to look at for inspiration. Grow rich, become financially secure, make something of yourself. I am embarrassed to say that a large bit of my treasure here on earth during my real estate career became what was on that personal financial statement.

Go Find that Field!

I want to return once again to the rich man who got it right in Matthew 13:44 because perhaps this passage contains the shortest yet most pound-for-pound effective teaching of all time. Jesus seems to strip away everything and present the Gospel to us in its most basic form. He says so clearly:

> *"The kingdom of heaven is like a treasure buried in a field, which a person finds and hides again, and out of joy goes and sells all he has and buys that field."*

I love this passage for so many reasons, but perhaps the main reason is the mention of this man's joy. The man isn't guilted into selling what he has. He is not shamed by God for what he has. Jesus doesn't ask him or even tell him that he needs to sell all he has. The man simply, and pretty quickly, and with great joy, realizes that Jesus is far better than everything else he has in his life. Jesus is better! Have you ever felt that way? Jesus is better than his plans. Jesus is better than his 401K. Jesus is better than his security, his retirement, his money, and his possessions. Jesus is better. So often I forget that Jesus is better, and I find myself running around pursuing things other than Him.

Some of us will spend a lifetime pursuing these things wholeheartedly while convincing ourselves that they are not keeping us from Jesus and from building His kingdom. Do you think the apostles in the early Church or any of the great saints spent their lives accumulating things on earth? This man gladly trades it all with joy, and he is not even asked to do so. How I long to emulate this man, yet how often I fall short. How I long to have so much joy in my heart for Jesus and His kingdom that I could follow in this man's steps. For this man, Jesus is the treasure, and He wants nothing else at all. He seems to understand that by seeking first true and lasting treasure everything else will fall into place (Matthew 6:33).

That first real estate deal set me on a course. It was a course of accumulation and a pursuit of financial security and treasure. I kept updating my personal financial statement, kept looking at it, and kept focusing on it. I was surrounded by so many people who did the same. Many people will tell you that this type of life is no problem at all. We have essentially labeled it "The American Dream." Accumulate the home and items that make you happy while preparing to secure *treasure* for your retirement; that way, you can sleep easy at night and hand something on to your children and grandchildren when you die.

I realize that I have bought into this American Dream like *it* is the treasure in the field. My life sometimes reflects this type of belief. Just stop and think about how much we work and live for financial treasure and security, but isn't it intriguing that these things are not really of interest to Jesus in the Gospels? In stark contrast, he is constantly rebuking many of the things I am tempted to pursue. Read the Gospels through again with the American Dream in mind. Is Jesus calling us to the American Dream, or is he calling us to something far greater?

Most days, I try to rise early to pray and read because, with six kids, it is the only time I can carve out to do so. I get so consumed and easily distracted by the many tugs at my mind and heart throughout the day. Many days this is the only time I have before people will be at our door or in the street presenting their needs to us.

The world is enormous, some seven-billion-plus huge, and the spiritual and physical needs of people are even greater. You and I live in one small corner of this world, but it is an important corner of the world because God and His children are living there with us.

How will I spend my days and nights? My life is extremely short, and the call to love God and our neighbor wholeheartedly is constant. When we lived in rural Central America, many days, people were knocking at our door just as the sun was rising. In just a couple of hours, children's stomachs will be growling once again in impoverished areas of Asia and Africa. As I type these words early this morning in my home, I can hear the call of Fajr, Muslim morning prayer, belting out into the streets around me. Just as clearly as these Muslims prayers belt out throughout my day here, I know that Jesus is inviting many of us to abandon all and build His kingdom so that those who hunger and thirst for Him, but do not know Him, would be able to receive Him. I know that Jesus is crying out to me to make Him my only treasure. But I can become so tangled up in my little dreams, and I can get so caught up polishing and updating my own little treasures.

In just a few moments, my children will arise and the day will start. There will be knocking at the door with people in need. No food, no mattress to sleep on, no job, drank too much cerveza last night, had no water to drink last night, need money for the bus, no home, no shoes, no rice, and on and on it goes. Along with these many requests, I will also be bombarded by the many allures this world has to offer me. If I don't rise early to pray and read scripture, then I have absolutely nothing to give. I must be reminded who and where my treasure is. If I don't speak with God early and often, then I lose sight of my treasure, Jesus.

Silver and Gold

While we lived in Central America, we were constantly viewed as the richest people in town, and rightly so, because we were. Although we are 100 percent dependent upon donations to live, we still have more than everyone there. Although we had given up much in our life back in America, to these beautiful people, we were still so rich. Because we have such generous mission partners, we were able to build homes for people, repair their roofs, install flooring for them, and feed them weekly. Though I know we helped them tremendously, I always felt a great desire and need to dig deeper and show them that their deepest desire, their deepest treasure, is Jesus. That they, like St. Augustine, could cry out, "Our hearts are restless, Oh God, until they rest in you."[9]

I haven't arrived at anything once I have a great, new sparkling house, or for these people a concrete floor. I haven't arrived anywhere once my belly is full, and I know where my next meal is coming from. My true arrival is knowing that I have no lasting treasure in this entire world except for Jesus Christ. Living and serving among the poor can be downright exhausting. Many times, Lacy and I were not equipped to serve the physical needs of the people knocking at our door in Costa Rica, but we always were able to point to Jesus and say, "I have an even greater treasure for you! His name is Jesus!"

While living in rural Costa Rica, we felt the Holy Spirit moving us to feed people. Initially, we didn't quite know how to follow through on this prompting, but we kept praying and waiting for God to speak clearly to us. One day, while on a long, tiresome run to a neighboring village, I realized He was inviting us to open a small center to feed the hungry of our town.

Coopevega is a small, poor, migrant farming town of about five hundred people. Many people there struggle to find work, thus food can become sparse for some families, especially outside of the harvest season. We opened the doors every Saturday evening about two hours before Mass. We invited everyone in town for a free meal, accompanied with prayer, songs, a testimony, a Gospel reading, and a small reflection of the Gospel reading. Our kids served (and often spilled) the food and drinks, and Lacy and I usually gave a Gospel reflection in our questionable Spanish.

Despite our weaknesses and shortcomings, week by week, the numbers grew as people were clearly hungry and willing to accept a free meal. However, what amazed me the most was how deeply spiritually hungry all of our new friends were. We met people who had journeyed from violent towns in Nicaragua, and we met people who had lived in the same small homes in Coopevega for years. We had drunks show up alongside old ladies who probably spent more time in their Bibles than I did. But they all came because of a deep hunger. They hungered and longed for Jesus, who is our true and lasting food, our true and lasting treasure.

As we served them and encountered them every week, many of them begged us to fill their many needs.

"Do you have shoes for my son or money for baby formula?"

"Can you build me a house or fix my roof?"

Some nights the requests went on and on. At times it was exhausting. We often had to stop them in their asking and declare to them like Peter boldly declared in Acts 3:6, "I have neither silver nor gold, but what I do have I give, in the name of Jesus the Nazorean, rise and walk."

I have found that I also have to stop myself dead in my requests and allow God to remind me that there will never be a time in my life when silver and gold is my greatest treasure. It will never satisfy me. In the same way that my new friends could only be satisfied with the treasure of Christ, you and I can't find our ultimate satisfaction outside of Him either.

Apostolic Witness

Each one of us, by virtue of our baptism and confirmation, is called to bear apostolic witness. That is, we are called to bear witness, or example, to the truth and goodness of the Gospel of Jesus Christ in a world that is passing and fading. In short, we are called to make it known to the world that Jesus Christ is our treasure.

The prophet Isaiah states it this way, "Your name and renown are the desire of our hearts" (Isaiah 26:8). Do I feel this deep desire within me, and do I desire for the name of Jesus to be great among those I live with? Do I desire His name to be great and renowned among the nations? Do I long to be a witness and reminder that Jesus Christ is love and mercy? What do people conclude about my God and His goodness by watching me live my life? Would they walk away and say that Jesus is one among many important parts of my life, or could they boldly declare that He is my only lasting treasure?

One of my personal heroes is Saint Pope John Paul II. He gifted the Church with an undeniable evangelical witness as he managed to log more miles traveling and preaching the Gospel than any other pope in our Church's history. It was he who so wholeheartedly began his letter Redemptoris Missio (Mission of the Redeemer) with the following words:

> *"The mission of Christ the Redeemer, which is entrusted to the Church, is still very far from completion. As the second millennium after Christ's coming draws to an end, an overall view of the human race shows that this mission is still only beginning."*[10]

Imagine that, more than 2,000 years removed from the life and death of Christ, and we are only just beginning as a Church. This is great news and terrible news at the same time. It is great news because it declares to us once again that now is the time to bear witness to the world, and you and I are still alive to be a part of it. A world that is hurting, longing, and lost. Now is the time to show the world our true treasure, Jesus. It is terrible news because it also sheds light on the truth that as a Church, we have often turned inward and failed in many ways.

Often I have failed to point people to this treasure that is Jesus Christ. Somehow, in a world of constant broadcasting and streaming, I have failed to fruitfully broadcast Jesus Christ to the nations who do not know Him. I have failed in so many ways to identify Jesus in the lost, poor, and hungry. People have walked away from interacting with me and not clearly understood who my treasure is. For St. John Paul II, the evidence of his life's treasure was made immensely visible throughout his twenty-six-year papacy. The selfless shepherd traveled to 129 different countries and logged more than a million miles making his treasure known to the world. For him, the name and renown of the Lord was a sole priority, his sole treasure.

What and where is your treasure? In Matthew 6:20, Jesus declares, "for where your treasure is, there also will your heart be."

What consumes your heart every day? What consumes your time and your money?

One day, about a year before I got out of business, I was shown a feature on my smartphone, whereby I could track every single mile I logged each day so long as I had my phone on me. I was shocked, and my treasure came into perspective. I could see many familiar places on my daily route: my home, do I really eat at that restaurant that much, my children's school parking lot.

But there was an undeniable pattern I could trace in my daily routine. The routine was to my office in the early morning, to several properties that we owned and managed, to the bank to make deposits and payments, back to my office, and back home. These were my days. Of course, I did other things, and there were other location pings each day, but these locations formed a giant, bold square. These four locations showed me where my treasure was. I was a little embarrassed honestly. There weren't many locations on there that did not involve some sort of exchange of money in my favor. Money had slowly become my treasure. I wouldn't have considered myself greedy per se, but my smartphone revealed evidence otherwise.

What consumes your days and nights? Is your smartphone record going to look more like Saint John Paul II's or like mine used to look? I am not saying there is anything inherently bad with going to work, making money, and supporting a family. These are good, necessary, and noble pursuits. But the question we must constantly (as in every single day) ask ourselves is: Is Jesus my sole treasure? Am I anything like the man who, out of joy, sold all he owned to find Jesus and His kingdom in that field? The world will continue to see through our American Prosperity version of Christianity until we are willing and able to trade all we have joyfully for Jesus Christ.

St. Paul, Rubbish, and the Ecuador Five

Perhaps the greatest bearer of apostolic witness can be found in St. Paul, and his life is worth examining when it comes to making Christ our one true treasure. It was St. Paul who boldly exclaimed, "whatever gains I had, these I have come to consider a loss, because of Christ. More than that, I even consider everything as a loss because of the supreme good of knowing Christ Jesus my Lord" (Philippians 3:7-8). Some translations replace the word loss with the word rubbish, and I love that verbiage. St. Paul considers every gain he ever had as rubbish when compared to knowing his treasure, Christ Jesus. Wow.

These words are strong and cannot be taken lightly. St. Paul has introduced a new standard for what is good and worthwhile. My new car: rubbish. A promotion and a raise: rubbish. What about financial security upon retirement?: rubbish. Again these things aren't rubbish on their own. But, in light of knowing Jesus Christ our Lord: rubbish. When the world sees us forgo these alluring earthly treasures for the sake of the Kingdom of God, they will ask us, why do you treasure Jesus so much? Explain to me why He is so worthy. Then they will want to spend time with the one who is worthy to be treasured.

Perhaps Fr. Thomas Dubay states it best regarding our apostolic witness when he says:

> *"If we wonder why, despite the millions of us who follow Christ, the world has not long ago been converted, we need not look far for one solution. We are not perceived as men on fire. We look too much like everyone else. We appear to be compromisers, people who say that they believe in everlasting life but actually live as though this life is the only one we have."*[11]

Oh, how I long to love and value Jesus with a heart so undivided. In the grand scale of eternity, my lifespan is but a small blip, and eternity with Him awaits me. Why would I want to get so bogged down in what is going on here in this short life?

The work *Through Gates of Splendor* by Elisabeth Elliot documents a group of men on fire who certainly understood Jesus Christ as their supreme treasure: Nate Saint, Jim Elliot, and the Ecuador Five.[12] The year was 1956, and these ambitious missionaries had long ago decided that their one true and lasting treasure was Jesus Christ and Him alone. Their hearts were dead set on Ecuador, namely the Huaorani tribe in Ecuador. No other human group had truly made contact with this tribe, as fear plagued anyone who dared even to ponder. The Huaorani tribe was a cannibalistic tribe, and they despised any outside human contact to the point of killing unwanted visitors and inquirers.

But the Lord of the universe had another plan, and had set these men's hearts ablaze. Jim Elliot and Nate Saint seem to have obtained most of the notoriety from this mission, but there were five brave men on board. They had been sharply warned not to approach this crazy group of cannibals for fear of their own lives. But the Holy Spirit was at work, and these men understood what St. Paul meant when he wrote, "Let those as having wives act as not having them. For the world, as we know it, is fading . . ." (1 Corinthians 7:29).

A movie entitled “End of the Spear,” which based on Elisabeth Elliot’s work, highlights the amazing scene of the men boarding a small plane to make their landfall and, hopefully, bring the good news of the Gospel to this dying tribe. The scene depicts them ascending into the air and the pilot glancing over at Nate Saint stating, "You know that you will die doing this?" To which Nate Saint boldly replied, "Sir, we died before we left."[13]

The gentlemen touched down and proceeded to set up camp and gain their surroundings. Initially, they assumed they made a fairly decent first impression as they received somewhat of a welcome by the tribe. But merely hours later, each one of them was brutally speared to death in the middle of the jungles of Ecuador. Every last one of them speared to death so soon after the impetus of their mission. I have personally spent a good bit of time reflecting on this scene and often wonder what ran through their minds as a spear punctured their skin and quickly darted into their hearts. When I consider their death, I often ask the following: *What were their final thoughts? Did they scream out praying? Did they doubt what they were doing?*

Back home in America, many people must have begged the question, "Why did these fools go to this God-forsaken place and reach out to these animalistic people?" To the world, they looked like fools. Fools who failed to calculate the cost of putting their lives at risk. Fools who had now abandoned their wives and children at home.

But I can only imagine a beautiful scene as they finally saw Jesus face to face. Can you picture that incredible scene? I mean seriously try to imagine it for a moment: just moments ago, they had absolutely no ground to stand on and no hope except for the promise of their dear Savior who whispered into their ear, "Do not fear or be dismayed" (Deuteronomy 31:8). "They that hope in the Lord will renew their strength" (Isaiah 40:31). "I will strengthen you and help you" (Isaiah 41:10). "The Lord your God is in your midst, a mighty savior" (Zephaniah 3:17). "Not a hair on your head will be destroyed" (Luke 21:18). And, "I am with you always until the end of the age" (Matthew 28:20). The only hope and the only treasure these men had was Jesus and His promises. Jesus was their treasure, and everything else was rubbish.

They now stood in front of Jesus face to face and heard him say, "Well done good and faithful servant . . . come, share your master's joy"(Matthew 25:23). Just imagine that. One moment they stared death in the eye of a spear, and the very next breath, they stood in glory and triumph before their Lord. They received the martyr's welcome into paradise where forever they will taste and see the goodness of the Lord they just laid down their lives for. What a glorious day! What a glorious scene!

Jim Elliot is known to have written in his journal before his death, "He is no fool who gives up that which he cannot keep to keep that which he cannot lose."[14] This is treasure. These are a group of men who joyfully gave up all they had to obtain their only treasure, Jesus Christ.

And of course, their apostolic witness did not fizzle out on the day of their death. Elisabeth Elliot, the wife of Jim Elliot, later returned to evangelize the Huaorani tribe, bringing many of them to faith in Jesus Christ, even some of the very men who took her husband's life. Their apostolic witness will forever be a consuming fire in the hearts of the Christian faithful who seek to spread the Kingdom of God amongst those most in need. Their apostolic witness is one of men on a temporary trek through this life with hearts and eyes on the final prize, Jesus. Where your heart is, there also lies your treasure.

I have no personal financial statement anymore, or at least I haven't updated it in several years. It would look pretty bad these days. Somewhere, I have kept a hard copy of it, and it is in a folder with the rest of our precious belongings. I keep it as a memory of something I used to hold near and dear to me. An old treasure that has now been replaced for something greater. We no longer own all that real estate, and I imagine that my phone tracking would look a bit different now.

Jesus is my treasure. I still mess it up all the time, though, and I mean that sincerely. Some days I would rather stay home and rest than visit our friends at the AIDS center, and some days, I am lured in to think that I can find my permanent treasure here in the world. It can be alluring. I still trade temporary treasures for the only treasure that remains, Jesus.

Lord, teach us to trade all our treasures in for you, the only treasure. For in doing so, we find you in all your fullness, and our lives will speak of your glory and goodness to all we encounter.

Chapter 6: Comfort

"Mount Calvary is the academy of love."[15]

– St. Frances de Sales

Ask my wife; she can tell you best. Most nights, I would just rather have a couple of drinks, eat a steak, and sit in an overstuffed chair watching basketball. The problem is that there is too much going on around me in the world to spend too much time doing that. The truth is that we live in a broken and lost world, and now is not the time for me to pursue comfort. I can experience that much later. I feel like such a hypocrite writing this, but now is not the time to pursue comfort. In Costa Rica, we slept under bug nets, took cold showers, and grunted and bore our way through heat rashes, but it simply became the norm for us. Please don't pat us on the back.

I will never forget the first time I returned to the United States after spending our first year serving as foreign missionaries outside of the United States of America. I drove through a beautiful, newly developed neighborhood. The houses were immaculate and perfectly manicured, most with two to four brand new cars resting in the fancy cobblestone driveways. The portable bathrooms for the construction workers were far nicer than some of the permanent bathrooms I had experienced elsewhere that year, and the neighborhood roads were far smoother than the national highways we drove. It was as if the sun was shining brighter in this neighborhood. The trees seemed greener and the grass seemed softer than the rest of the world.

I wasn't indicting the people who lived in this neighborhood. I was only struggling personally to settle with the fact that such a small group of people had such an abundance of comforts while such a large group of people had none. I felt really out of place driving through this lovely development; one I had driven through many times before. I now had the eyes of the poor. I almost felt like they were sitting in the passenger seat with me with their jaws on the ground. I imagined how my poor neighbors in rural Costa Rica would view this place. They would pass out. My head spun. It hurt to even think about it.

It seems like I spend most of my life pursuing something I can never obtain, and in the end, even what I have obtained will be gone in an instant. "A puff of smoke that appears briefly and then disappears" (James 4:14). At some point, I was told or came to believe that the best way to exist on this earth is through extreme comfort, and so I tend to seek it. Constantly. Think about your own day.

The clothes I wear, the food I eat, the cars I drive, the chairs I sit in, the homes I live in. I seek comfort. It is ingrained in me. I remember when we purchased our "dream home" in America in our dream neighborhood. We spent so much precious time pondering what color floors would match the walls and what type of flowers would match the trees. We found fluffy couches to sit on for the few hours we were actually at home. Within two years, God would generously invite us to leave it all behind. In a moment's notice, none of it really mattered.

True Comfort versus Every Comfort in the World

True comfort comes through Jesus Christ and His promises. True comfort is knowing the Father's love and His constant desire to provide every need and longing we have. True comfort is looking at the seductive lures of this world and walking in the other direction, holding fast to the Father's love. It's hard to do. The world offers us comfort as well. It is often intoxicating and easy, but it is fool's gold and short-lived. We all have tasted it.

When we lived in Coopevega, there were beautiful yet exhausted people constantly arriving from Nicaragua. Some of them journeyed through the night or several days and arrived there with simply a bag of belongings. Many of them would pile into small houses comprised of many families living together, just trying to find a small, thin mattress for everyone to lie on. I often envy their simplicity and their lack of excess. Their country has been rattled and torn by horrible violence. Their schools are closing down as bullets whiz by their children's earlobes. They have no hope or comfort in this world.

Here in Asia, we have encountered many Rohingyan refugees who have been violently driven out of their country of Myanmar in a current-day ethnic cleansing. They have fled several countries over seeking refuge with their young and innocent children in tow. Theirs is an identity of absolutely no earthly shelter or comfort, as even their own government leaders have violently driven them out of their homes. They are always on the run, simply searching for a bit of stability and justice for their families.

I believe, in their simplicity and humility, these people embody how Jesus wants us to live as disciples when scripture says, "He instructed them to take nothing for the journey but a walking stick—no food, no sack, no money in their belts" (Mark 6: 7-9).

Sometimes I view this type of existence as impossible in our current day and age, but these are the words of Jesus to the men who would go out and change the world. I believe one of the greatest hindrances in my life keeping me from getting closer to Jesus is my union with the comforts of this world. It is fleeting, but for some reason, I keep chasing after it. Jesus tells us we can't love both the world and Him, and that we will end up despising one or the other (1 John 2:15). So which one do we despise?

If we were to take an objective and outside look on the majority of modern-day Christianity, sometimes what we will find is guidance to make us thrive in our world today. And certainly thriving today as a human in this world holds its place of importance, but it is not the end goal. So often we receive the message that to thrive in this life is the end goal.

Sometimes I settle for a Gospel of therapy instead of a Gospel of the death, life, and resurrection with Jesus Christ. But it quickly leads me down the road of the Almighty American Dream, whereby I am solely pursuing "my best life" now and asking Jesus to help me get there. I think I have arrived at my destination when I no longer have a mortgage on my dream home, and I find such comfort in a pay raise at work. I eagerly long all year for a Christmas bonus or a family vacation. I place so much stock in earthly comfort.

But for the disciple of Jesus Christ, none of these things matter. The true disciple of Christ is indifferent to these things. He or she can either enjoy the vacation at the end of the year or not, but the entire year will not be spent thinking about it. The true disciple longs to be with Jesus in eternity where true, lasting comfort will exist. But I can get so caught up in prosperity here on earth. But this idea as a whole is missing in the Gospels. Sure, Jesus wants us to experience comfort and lasting joy, but it is not found in the world.

"Are we missionaries when every comfort is ours?"[16]

– Fr. Thomas Dubay

When we first moved to rural Costa Rica, we lived in a three-bedroom home that was built for us by our landlord. The home was new and was built to accommodate a large family. It was new and nice, but by American standards, it was a challenge for us to live in. There was no air conditioning, hot water was in and out at times, and we had to hang-dry our laundry outside. For the first few months, I found myself longing for these comforts that I was so accustomed to while I lived in the United States: air conditioning, hot water, a clothes dryer, a microwave, a toaster.

After a few months, the local people we served began visiting us in our home. Every one of them would exclaim, "What a large and nice home you have! Wow, you have a refrigerator, an oven, a bathroom, and even a clean private water well!" I was humbled so quickly.

The luxury items I had given up did not even register for these people because most of them had never experienced life with a clothes dryer or an air conditioner. Most of them lived on dirt floors and had old and dirty water wells. Most of them lived in homes with large gaps between the planks of second and third-hand wood on their walls. Eventually, we realized that what we were internalizing as sacrificial living was viewed by most people in our town as luxury living. We felt like our witness was conflicting. In one breath, these people were hearing us exclaim, "We have left everything behind to serve God in a foreign land," but in another breath, they saw us living in one of the nicest homes in the entire town.

It took us a few months to realize that to these beautiful people, our evangelical witness was possibly being weakened simply by the home we were living in. In a very short time, we felt called to move out of this home and settle for something a little bit more like the average person in our town.

Perhaps the most striking witness of Christianity, especially for those outside of it, is that God became man, making His dwelling among us. He became one of us and lived with us. Jesus lived among us and was like us in every way except for sin. Anytime I have a good conversation about Jesus with someone who is not a Christian here in Asia, that seems to be the focal point. Jesus changed the meaning of what it means to be God for the entire world; He became man. That changed everything for the entire history of the world.

Can you imagine Jesus being subject to the cruelties and hardships of life: natural disasters, abuse, infidelity, and disease? He didn't live tucked away in His plush, secure quarters apart from frail humanity. Further, He got His start in a humble barn, even beneath the frailness of humanity. Jesus saw it all, yet tasted none of it. This is one aspect of Christianity that packs such an enormous punch. There is a certain witness we find in Jesus because He chose to find Himself among us, building His kingdom.

I have discovered the same profound evangelical witness can be found in us when we give up our comforts to live among those people God has called us to pursue. When we give up our comforts and earthly desire for the sake of the Kingdom of God, we cause people to ask the next question: "Why in the world would someone do that?"

In his book *Let the Nations Be Glad*, John Piper states:

> *"J. Oswald Sanders tells the story of an indigenous missionary who walked barefoot from village to village preaching the Gospel in India. His hardships were many. After a long day of many miles and much discouragement, he came to a certain village to speak the Gospel, but was driven out of town and rejected. So, he went to the edge of the village, dejected and lay down under a tree and slept from exhaustion. When he awoke, people were hovering over him, and the whole town was gathered around to hear him speak. The head man of the village explained that they came to look over him while he was sleeping.*

When they saw his blistered feet, they concluded that he must be a holy man and that they had been evil to reject him. They were sorry and wanted to hear the message that he was willing to suffer so much to bring them."[17]

Where is my evangelical witness? What am I willing to give up to reach a people lost and in need of Jesus? This willingness to leave our comforts for the sake of spreading the Gospel is central to our Christian faith. Am I willing to forgo some of my comforts for the sake of making His name great among those people Christ will call me to pursue? Even my greatest comforts. Even those comforts that are not bad?

Perhaps my problem is that I have simply been told all of my life that I just need to give up sin to follow Jesus? This is such a minimalistic approach. Yes, giving up sin to follow Jesus is an important step, but it is only the first step. What Jesus loudly proclaims to us at the beginning of the Gospels St. Paul echoes later in the acts of the Apostles: "Repent and believe in the Gospel!" (Mark 1:15). But unfortunately, I often view my Christian life as if this command is the beginning and the end. Then I find ways to indulge in my comforts, so long as they are not "sinful." But what about my witness? What about my destination being eternal and our treasure being stored up in heaven and not in barns where moth and decay can destroy (Matthew 6: 19-20)?

Have people seen the bottom of our feet? What do they look like? Have our feet ventured out of our comfort zone and into a land or street in need?

Far too often my feet have been sheltered and comforted in a land so familiar to me: my land of comfort. This is not the land of the apostles or their master, Jesus. To be a disciple calls my feet to venture outside of my comforts, to journey away from my couch, my phone, vehicle, or gated community. To be a disciple requires me to establish a new comfort level for myself; one not dictated by my own desires but dictated by the needs and desires of the hearts of the people God places before me.

We have friends, Beaux and Alix, who live and serve in Haiti, preaching the Gospel and serving the poor selflessly. They sold their large family farm in beautiful Colorado and ventured away from their known comforts to pursue beautiful people in great need. My friend, Beaux, enjoys fine whiskey and cigars but now settles for a cold Coke because that's all he can get in Haiti. That is now his earthly satisfaction at the end of the day. His eternal satisfaction is his Lord and King Jesus Christ, and his daily joy, comfort, and treasure is building the Kingdom of his King in Haiti. He has stripped himself of almost every single comfort he used to cling to and allowed his heavenly Father to provide satisfaction and comfort for him and his family. How blessed indeed are the feet of those who carry the good news (Romans 5:25).

The Grass and the Flowers

Perhaps some of this sounds a bit too intense? After all, doesn't God want us to be happy here on earth? He wants us to be happy, to experience true joy. But that true and lasting joy can only come from Him, and far too often the comforts of this world only leave me longing for more.

A personal hero and dear friend of mine named Lance always says the following: "When I finish my life, I want to barely be able to run across the finish line because I want to have spent giving away every single ounce of what God has given to me in service of Him and other people. Every ounce of what God has given me to build up His kingdom and His glory." Lance's thought always reminds me of my time running in Costa Rica. We had roughly fifty small pueblos or villages all separated by miles and miles of unpaved dirt and rock roads. Many of these people had no means of transportation and lived quite far off from much of civilization.

About once per week, I would strap on my camel pack, grab a banana and a Gatorade, and run off to a new pueblo or two and try to meet folks, try to share Christ with them. Every single time, without fail, I would find myself running back home afterward and worrying if I had enough water in my camel pack. Sometimes I would run up to fifteen or twenty miles, so I would start to panic thinking about the possibility of running out of water. But then I would think of my friend's quote: *just empty it out and don't worry about having reserves!*

I think that's how I am called to live on earth as a missionary disciple of Jesus Christ. Just empty it out before we cross the finish line. Don't worry about what we have for reserves; God can handle that part of it.

Put yourself out there. Be uncomfortable. Has He ever failed us? Without fail, each time, I would make it back home with just a sip or two of water. He always provides for us, especially when we remove ourselves from our comfort zone and empty our lives for Him and His Gospel. Imagine if we could apply that challenge to our lives as Christian disciples. Put ourselves out there for Jesus and His kingdom. To go way beyond our comfort levels when we commit to prayer, to loving others, to loving Jesus, to following His Commandments, receiving the sacraments, to sharing His Gospel.

Far too often, I am tempted to just look around and seek comfort like everyone else, and far too often, I am told by those around me (other Christians) that this is okay. But this was never Jesus' message in the Gospel. We see, quite the contrary, God constantly reminding us that this world is passing and that our time on earth is short. St. Peter reminds us as he declares, "For all flesh is like grass, and its glory like the flower of the field; the grass withers, and the flower wilts, but the word of the Lord remains forever" (1 Peter 1:24). And again, we are reminded in the letter of James, "You have no idea what your life will be like tomorrow. You are but a puff of smoke that appears briefly and then disappears" (James 4:14). So obviously the choice is ours. Will we continue to cling so tightly to these things that will burn and wither up so quickly?

When Lacy and I married, we emptied both of our savings accounts and purchased a condo. We completely renovated it, making it our own. We were so happy, comfortable, and content. *We can live here for the next ten years at least,* we thought.

Roughly six weeks later, on the day of my grandmother's funeral, a disaster occurred and an enormous fire broke out on the roof of our complex, completely damaging ten units. Ours was among the number that was burned down and then dowsed with thousands and thousands of gallons of water by the fire team. A complete loss, total devastation in our young marriage. We stood at the roadside watching our hopes and dreams go up in smoke half-dressed to attend a funeral. We had worked so hard, saved, lived responsibly, and had done it right, but now it was all gone.

I believe this is how our lives can go. Have you ever attended a funeral of someone who died unexpectedly and all too young? It can be a tragic occasion. Aside from the obvious and tender truth that someone's loved one has been ripped away from them, we often sit in our utter amazement that this person is now gone forever. This person, whom we thought and assumed would live for so much longer, is now gone from this earth. We let death catch us off guard, or assume it will never come for us. We spend most of our lives preparing more and more comfort here on earth, almost as if we are going to live here on earth forever. If God tells us that all flesh is all going to wither and wilt away like grass and flowers, why wouldn't we get a head start and begin to distance ourselves from it, and grab hold tighter to Him, the one whose love and comfort will never cease to exist?

Now, far removed from the pain of our fire, Lacy and I often look back on that moment and laugh. If only God would have called us into foreign missions at that point. It would have been so much easier. But that entire experience was a wake-up call for us. It taught us that everything we have, including one another, can be gone in an instant. We had many faithful and true family members and friends who helped us get back on our feet, but our creed became more simply defined. “In you, O Lord is my trust, never let me be put to shame” (Psalm 31:2).

I believe, in the end of our lives, we will be asked what or who is our ultimate comfort. I imagine that none of us will be able to escape this question from God, our Lord and Creator. Imagine that grand scene. You and God sitting back and watching the highlights and lowlights of your life. What will our answer be? What is your comfort? I also imagine that God won’t allow us to speak much, as we will have just spent our entire lifetimes speaking the answer to this question. We will just be able to look back on our lives with God and look at all the things we took comfort and refuge in throughout our lives.

I sometimes cringe at this thought, because I know how sinful and attached I am. Undoubtedly, we will all fall short, and that's where we need His grace today. I'm sure we will look back with God and say, "I’m sorry I was so stupid right there. Look at me. How shallow? Thanks for pulling me out of that stupid spot." But with God's opportunity for grace and forgiveness, today we can say those same things. Lord, I am so shallow and I repent of the ways I am finding such comfort in this world that is so quickly passing in front of me. Please forgive me and reset my heart and mind and align my desires with you.

You, O Lord, you are my comfort, my refuge, my only hope; all my hope is in you and you alone.

Chapter 7: Where's the Passion!

"If, then you are looking for the way by which you should go, take Christ, because He Himself is the way."[18]

– St. Thomas Aquinas

When was the last time you met someone with great passion? I was blessed to have a spiritual director named Fr. Philip Merdinger while I was in the seminary. He is the founder of a thriving religious community named The Brotherhood of Hope. When you encountered him in the hallways, you could almost grab a hold of his passion as if it were obtainable. He walks around with a mission, to mold young men into disciples of Jesus Christ. He was always on the lookout for his men, always looking to make eye contact with us and see how we were doing.

I recall one afternoon in the seminary when the season of Lent was approaching. This is usually a season people would rather sort of ease into as it generally will bring about some sacrifice and personal pruning. But here Fr. Philip was roaming the halls clapping his hands like a basketball coach in the last minute of a tied championship game calling out to each of us, "Lent is coming! Yes! Lent is almost here! Who is ready for Lent, brothers?!" An enormous enthusiasm overflowed from within him in his pursuit to draw closer to Jesus. This is passion. His passion was unavoidable; it was contagious. Amid apathy, mediocrity, and fear, passion enters the room and blows the doors down.

To go out into the whole world and make disciples, I must have great passion. St. Paul states in 1 Corinthians, "Do you not know that those who run in a race all run, but only one receives the prize? Run in such a way that you may win" (1 Cor 9:24). And again in the Letter to the Philippians, he claims that if there is any encouragement in Christ and any fellowship in the Holy Spirit for us, we must strive to have the same mind, love, spirit, and intention of purpose as he does (Philippians 2:1-2). That's an intense challenge. There are no saints along the way who have done so with great apathy. There is no patron saint of the mediocre and apathetic, and I don't think that's who God is calling me to become.

Yet sometimes if I take a pulse on myself and even our Church, I will discover a bunch of apathy and mediocrity. Sometimes, my response to Jesus is apathetic, my giving of myself and my resources can be apathetic, and thus my witness becomes very . . . apathetic. This is no way for me to live out the Great Commission with authenticity.

In his *Apostolic Exhortation Evangellii Gaudium* (The Joy of the Gospel), Pope Francis calls us to a renewed passion in our evangelical witness. He states:

> *"How I long to find the right words to stir up enthusiasm for a new chapter of evangelization full of fervor, joy, generosity, courage, boundless love and attraction. Yet I realize that no words of encouragement will be enough unless the fire of the Holy Spirit burns in our hearts."*[19]

In light of Pope Francis' words, I have to ask myself, *Where is my enthusiasm, fervor, joy, and attraction?* When is the last time someone entered my presence and thought, *Wow, I want what he has!?* Like Pope Francis, I believe that now is the time and our hearts are the place for this new evangelization to take place. I fear that the world looks at our apathetic brand of Christianity and wants little to do with it because it lacks a sincere authenticity, it lacks the Holy Spirit, and it lacks passion.

What is Passion?

To have passion means to be resolute and concise in accomplishing a task, doing so selflessly and with enthusiasm. The Latin root of the word passion is *patior*, which means to suffer.[20] To have passion for someone or something means we must be willing to suffer or lay down many things to accomplish that task which is most important. If I am passionate about my children, then I am willing to sacrifice and even suffer for them to bring the greatest good for them, and I am willing to do all of this with great enthusiasm.

In fact, enthusiasm is often the signature of having great passion. When a person exudes passion and enthusiasm, oftentimes a natural byproduct is confidence and authority. Jesus' life was one of enthusiasm, one of passion, and His passion was exemplified in His sacrificial death. For this reason, the scribes and Pharisees of His day were threatened. When Jesus spoke, people stopped to listen. "When Jesus finished these words, the crowds were astonished at his teaching, for he taught them as one having authority, and not as their scribes" (Matthew 7:29).

What Does Passion Look Like?

Some days it's easier to go through the motions out here and forget that I am running a race, and that God has called me to do so with a grand passion. It's easy to fall into the trap and view the Gospel as a burden or to see the Great Commission as something "I have to do." It can also be tempting to see the daily challenges of learning a new language, adapting into a new culture, and answering knocks on our door as a burden. But these are all given to me as an opportunity to strengthen my love and desire for Christ and His Church, to strengthen my passion. To grow in passion is to die to myself.

I can remember a period of a couple of months while living in Costa Rica when my spirits were low and my desire to serve was not at its best. It seemed like more and more people were coming to our door, knocking and asking for everything under the sun. "We need rice, we need beans, we need a mattress, we need a house. We have no bug nets, we have no water, and we have nothing but a dirt floor." I was just so exhausted and overwhelmed. I was most certainly going through the motions, and I was not seeing Christ in the eyes of the people I was serving; in some ways, they were becoming a burden to me.

I think my pity party came to a head one Saturday afternoon while we were preparing for one of our Feed the Hungry Nights. Every Saturday, we would prepare and serve roughly seventy people a free meal, share the Gospel, and pray with them. Of course, we were always scrambling to pull everything together every week, and I was wiped out. I had a talk prepared but was really doubting that it was worth a salt. I just wanted to punt on the entire night. I had no passion. As the evening started, I was pondering just serving the meal and telling everyone that we had no sharing or Gospel reflection for that evening. I am so ashamed to share that, but I believe I was just running on empty that night. I silently said a half-hearted prayer of desperation for God to help me out; even my prayer felt lifeless and devoid of passion.

All of the sudden, my phone rang and it was my dear friend Pablo. You will recall Pablo from another chapter as the man who sliced up a coral snake with his machete to save my daughter from being bitten. Pablo is like passion in a bottle; wherever he goes, you can sense the Holy Spirit. He is holy, faithful, and has died to himself in many ways in his lifetime. I told him we were starting our evening, and I sort of jokingly asked him if he would be willing to share his testimony over the phone with our group, because I felt like I had nothing to give.

To my surprise Pablo took my request seriously and demanded that I place the phone up to the microphone so he could share with the group. What transpired was an amazing and passion-filled testimony of how Jesus was there among them all and how Jesus had broken down walls in his life, walls of sin and shame, and that Jesus wanted to do the same in their lives. He shared with them how blessed they all were to have a night like this whereby God would meet them all in a humble meal and the Word of God. It was an amazing and inspiring five minutes. My soul was instantly revived, and I could see the passion these beautiful people had in their eyes to know, love, and follow Jesus deeper. I am certain that Pablo's sharing completely reshaped the outcome of our night. Praise God. As I hung up the phone, Pablo asked me to please call him back late that evening after we were finished serving.

I finally got around to calling Pablo late that night. I learned that he was actually calling me to ask for my prayers for a situation he was struggling with. Something was completely weighing down him and his family, and he needed help. But in that moment of my request, he was able to die to himself and his own needs and share the deep, life giving love of Jesus with us. I hung up the phone and thought, *this dude was dying on the inside, yet managed to deliver an inspiring sharing on the love of Christ on the spot.* This is passion, and on that night, I learned what it looked and sounded like. My dear friend Pablo has passion, and his passion restored mine on that night.

Passion looks like five men boarding a plane to Ecuador knowing they will probably be brutally speared and martyred by the very people they will reach out to. Passion looks like the eleven apostles scattering themselves across the world delivering the Gospel unto death when just weeks before they found themselves speechless in an upper room trying to figure where they would go from here. Passion looks like a frail, withering nun overflowing with humility named Teresa walking the slums of Calcutta, her body writhing in pain. Passion is exemplified in the life of St. Maximilian Kolbe giving his life away in a death chamber for another man he didn't even know.

Passion is seen in the life of Saint Paul who, after his great conversion, gave his entire life for the sake of the Gospel, enduring every trial imaginable. As he states in 2 Corinthians 11:24-27:

> *"Five times at the hands of the Jews I received forty lashes minus one. Three times I was beaten with rods, once I was stoned, three times I was shipwrecked, I passed a night and a day on the deep, on frequent journeys, in dangers from rivers, dangers from robbers, dangers from my own race, dangers from Gentiles, dangers in the city, dangers in the wilderness, dangers at sea, dangers among false brothers; in toil and hardship, through many sleepless nights, through hunger and thirst, through frequent fastings, through cold and exposure."*

It's easy for me to stand up once a week and deliver a talk or a teaching; it's also easy to claim I have a passion for Jesus and the Church at Christmas or during an annual retreat. It's easy to become passionate about a hot topic issue in the Church, like married priests or the appropriate language of a Mass, but Jesus is not calling me to waste my passions away on these things. Jesus is calling me to be passionate about making disciples of the entire world and to do so with great enthusiasm. So let's sit back and ask ourselves the question: where is my passion?

When we first started dating, my wife quickly discovered how insane I was. I generally watch Duke basketball games standing up. I know it's strange and childish. I'm working on it, and now that I don't have a television, it's much easier. But I was passionate about this trivial college basketball game. While dating, she bought us two tickets to go see Duke play Georgia Tech. We made an unbelievable weekend out of it. It came time for the game, and of course, I stood up in front of a bitter and losing Georgia Tech fan. The entire game he screamed at me to sit down, and the entire game I was about one foot from pushing this man and telling him to shut up. I'm now embarrassed to say that I was so passionate about that game.

We become passionate about politics, passionate about sports, and passionate about succeeding in our careers. We have people who stand on street corners during election season passionately holding up signs about their favorite candidate. There are people who pay for season tickets to their favorite sports team, spend thousands of dollars during a weekend on events leading to and chasing the weekly game, and then plan their following week around next week's game. They are passionate about their team.

And let me not just point the finger because oftentimes my passion is misplaced as well. For years my passion was success. Remember, I had goals to be financially independent and retired by the age of fifty, and I did my best to dedicate loads and loads of time in this passionate pursuit. I woke up on many Saturday mornings at 4:45 and headed to my office to work because I knew I would be the only one in my industry doing this and believed this would get me ahead. We are all passionate about something: Is it Jesus? Is it His mandate to us to go into all the world and make disciples?

For some reason, I believe that there is some imaginary line drawn in the sand, and if I cross it, then I am seen as having too much passion for Christ. It is real. Sometimes I am afraid to have too much of Jesus. If we are honest and we take the time to read the Gospels, we will see men and women who encountered Him, and they were left with great passion; they were forever changed. As I read these encounters and consider all of the life changing encounters I have had with Christ, I can conclude with great certitude: Jesus is worth all of my passion. Few people in the Gospels encounter Jesus and walk away apathetic. But many times, I can encounter Jesus every single week in the Eucharist and walk away apathetic, and I just can't imagine that is okay in the eyes of God. This is not the model given to us in the Gospel.

The Passion of Jesus

I often pray prayers like, "Lord, give me a deeper and greater passion for you." And those prayers are excellent, but have we ever stopped to ask Jesus Himself what His deepest passions are? Have we ever spent time in the Gospels with an eye on what makes Jesus come alive? If I wanted to find out your passions, what drives you, I could simply follow you around and see what you spend your time on, what websites you visit when you are free, what goals you have, what makes you cry, and where you draw your joy from. We can observe the same things in Jesus.

We can draw every conclusion we need to know about the passion of Jesus Christ from His sacrificial action upon the cross. Unlike us, all of His actions leading up to and going from His death on a cross are all of the same accords. When Jesus approached His death in Gethsemane, he cried out in deep, deep despair "not my will, but yours be done" (Luke 22:42).

So what is the Father's will? The Father's will for us, all 7 billion of us, is to taste eternal glory for all eternity and for us to give that away. For this reason, Jesus endured death on a cross. Everything he did up to that point is paramount. It proclaimed the heart and passion of Jesus. Before His death, He proclaimed the kingdom of God (to the poor); He cured the sick, raised the dead, instructed His apostles, and made disciples. This was all an enormous expression of self-giving love. This is the heart of Jesus.

If I long to model my life around the passion of Jesus, then there it is. Am I excited, enthusiastic, about these things? This is where Jesus' time, energy, and heart went while He was on earth. He is the example.

After His death, Jesus saw a need to reiterate His passion to us as He gathered His closest apostles and sent them out to do the exact same thing that He did, "Go into all the world and proclaim the Gospel to every creature" (Mark 16:15). Jesus' passion was proclaimed in His life, His death, and in His resurrection, and it was done perfectly. Jesus is the perfect example of the heart and passion of God.

I once met a man who accumulated millions and millions of dollars and was nowhere near stopping his accumulation. He had worked extremely hard, met the right people, and invested well. He was close to being a billionaire. He was a Christian like me. He had a great passion that was contagious when I sat with him. When I left his presence, I wanted to become more successful and work harder. His passion was his success, his assets, his family, and his wealth, and they were abundant. He was an honest and forthright man and a pleasure to be around. However, the passions of Christ—the lost, the poor, the unreached—were far from his heart.

Perhaps you are like me, and if we are honest with ourselves, we can hold up a mirror to that man and see ourselves. We believe in Jesus and want Jesus in so far as He doesn't interfere with or keep us from our other passions. And most of all, there are times in our lives where Jesus is not our supreme passion. We sort of fit the passions and desires of Jesus into our lives where convenient. We are on a road of fulfillment for ourselves, a road toward success in the eyes of the world. But if and when we truly examine the life of Jesus Christ, we will see His life was nothing at all like my friend's life.

Jesus didn't work in His passion for the salvation of the lost and justice for the poor when it was convenient. He worked them in at the cost of His entire life. He abandoned any thought or desire to pursue His agenda and submitted it all to His Heavenly Father who sent Him to die. We see the same common thread with the first apostles of Jesus. We see men leave their nets and family businesses, drop their plans and aspirations, all in hopes to fulfill the plan and passion of Jesus.

I've never met a priest like Fr. Philip. So humble, yet so passionate. One night, I ventured into the chapel at the seminary late at night because I could not sleep. It must have been 3 a.m. And there he was before the Blessed Sacrament praying passionately. I could sense in his voice that he was struggling with something. Yet there he was instead of indulging in himself or what the world had to offer; he was dying to himself and gaining the passion of Christ right before the Blessed Sacrament. Passion is an amazing thing. When you see it, you know it, and it tends to stick with you. Where is your passion?

Chapter 8: Why Follow Jesus?

"Apart from the cross, there is no other ladder by which we may get to heaven."[21]

– St. Rose of Lima

When we moved to Southeast Asia to serve, we settled into an apartment somewhat in the middle of town. The very week we moved in, a "Hindu roadside temple" was being erected right behind our place. It was amazing to see the bright purple, orange, and yellow colors blended together upon their Hindu statues; many of the Hindu gods were represented. My children asked every question under the sun about what these men were doing working day and night to complete the temple. From our apartment view, we could see them working tirelessly day and night, even sleeping outside under tarps at night. Then finally, the temple opened and there was a week-long celebration of food, festival, and prayer in our backyard each night. Loud, beautiful chanting and music with new, bright rhythms kept our kids awake on their pillows as they pondered where in the world their parents had taken them.

Once we visited Thailand only to realize it was the feast of the Celebration of Lights. Apparently, on this night, everyone was purchasing large luminaries that they would release into the sky. They offered up the luminaries as a prayer to the goddess of the water, the Hindu goddess Ganga, seeking to offer her thanksgiving. It was a beautiful celebration, but I found myself standing there looking up at these beautiful lights wondering if these people believed there was a goddess of water. Did they believe that a goddess of a river could help them or others in any way? As we returned home, the luminaries were beginning to tumble down from the sky, heavily plopping upon the pavement covered in smoke. I wondered if this meant that their prayers were answered or unheard.

As a Catholic, I have often found myself pondering the many religions of the world and their significance. Although I have studied world religions, I have lived much of my life in an American Catholic town, rarely being exposed to the reality of other religions. However, where we now reside is a Muslim dominant country, and we have come to learn so much about the Islam faith, everything from fasting to constant call to prayer booming out through the streets. There are always other religions present here; it is not uncommon for us to engage with Hindus, Taoists, Muslims, and Chinese Free Thinking Atheists in one day. It is a melting pot of Asian culture and religion, and in the East, the spiritual always seems to be on display.

As missionaries, we have been exposed to the sheer enormity of the world, and we have seen so many beautiful people all sincerely seeking to find God. It has been a blessing to have the opportunity to present Jesus as the focal point of all of man's religions. It can be such an enormous challenge, though, but it runs so deeply in our hearts and veins. For some people, our presentation of Christ has been the first sincere presentation to them in their lives.

You may remember my friend Basri from earlier, first room on the right as we walk into the AIDS Home, bedridden, coiled up, withering away, and dying from the AIDS virus. I have really come to be at peace with him, sitting on a chair next to his bedside. Because of religious restrictions, I had to protect my family and myself and not do anything too stupid. So for many weeks, I just sat quietly with him and prayed that God would show His face to Basri in His perfect time.

As my visits with Basri added up, I began to ponder deeply on the following questions: *Does it matter if Basri ever hears the*

Gospel of Jesus Christ? Does Jesus have anything to offer Basri that no one else can offer him?

Googling Jesus

One day here in Asia, I took an Uber ride to a meeting at a cafe across town. I generally try to initiate some sort of meaningful conversation with my drivers. I just pray that the Holy Spirit will guide my conversation and that I can be a witness to love.

After questioning him about his Buddhist faith for a little while, the man turned to me and asked me if I believed in God. I told him I believed in Jesus and that Jesus was my God. There was somewhat of a language barrier, so he kept asking me to repeat myself.

"Jesus, Jesus," I said. "I believe in Jesus, have you heard of Him?" He continued to question what I was saying, and eventually, he grabbed his phone and had me type in what I was saying.

“Oh, Jesus, like the man they said died . . .”

“Yes sir, that's Him!” I said. “That’s my Lord!”

He allowed me to "give an explanation for my hope in Jesus" (1 Peter 3:15), and so I did so with great joy. He was blown away that the God I worship actually became man, lived among us, suffered, died, and rose from the dead for the price of our redemption and salvation. For him, with a Buddhist background, this idea of a god being able to do this was a mind-blowing idea.

At some point in our lives, we have to come to grips with the fact that what God has done in and through Jesus Christ is indeed mind blowing and life changing. Either that, or as C.S. Lewis proposes, Jesus was a liar or a lunatic.[22]

In all of the history of the religions of the world, there has never been a God to pursue our lost and broken humanity in such a reckless and loving way. No other God has humbled Himself so selflessly "emptying himself out" and "taking the form of a slave" (Philippians 2:7) in order to pursue a people He loves so immensely. No other God comes close to pursuing His lost children with such ferocity and love as Jesus does.

We see this so clearly in the parables of the lost sheep, the lost coin, and the lost son, all conveniently found side by side in Luke 15. Here we see the true heart of Jesus. He longs for and desires us, His lost children, and He will not spare and did not spare anything to find us and to reconcile us to His Father. Each one of us matters to Him because we all belong to Him. In spite of our sinfulness and shortcomings “while we were still sinners” (Romans 5:8), Jesus is found pursuing us, His lost sons and daughters, and even running toward us to embrace us (Luke 15:20) with His mercy and grace. This is the heart and character of God. This is Jesus.

As I continue to grow older, I can relate more and more to the lost Son who is at the end of his rope and finally plans his return home to his Father. I sense that God, my Father, is always running toward me even in the midst of my failures. Furthermore, it seems that when I truly blow it big time, He is running after me all the more.

Sadly, we now live in a world that believes that Jesus is just another potential remedy among many other remedies. Like, if I want to lose weight, I can become a vegan or a carnivore, I can try to exercise or not, or I can even fast. It doesn't matter which path I choose, though, because all paths will bring me to my desired end. But it is not the case with God.

This form of religious relativism is addressed by Pope John Paul II in his Redemptoris Missio when he states that "it is based on incorrect theological perspectives and is characterized by a religious relativism which leads to the belief that one religion is as good as another."[23] Indeed, the Church believes that all people both "stem from and share a common destiny towards God"[24]; what God does in Jesus Christ is unparalleled, and this truth changes everything. God reminds us time and again in scripture how broken, lost, and sinful we are and, more importantly, the grave consequences of our sin (Romans 3:23; Romans 6:23). We all stand in need of a savior, someone who can reunite us to God our Father, someone who can bridge the gap for us.

Scripture tells us that in the fullness of time, God sent His one and only son into the world to redeem us (Galatians 4:4-7). This was God's loving and merciful plan to reconcile us to Himself. Jesus is the ransom and mediator. Only Jesus. The Church so beautifully declares:

> *"The sacrifice of Christ is unique; it completes and surpasses all other sacrifices. First, it is a gift from God the father Himself, for the Father handed his Son over to sinners in order to reconcile us with Himself. At the same time it is the offering of the Son of God made man, who in freedom and love offered his life to his Father through the Holy Spirit in reparation for our disobedience."*[25]

If we are to speak of a God of any type, then we are to speak of Jesus at some point. He is absolutely unavoidable.

Perhaps what amazes me the most in Jesus is that reading through the Gospels attentively, you will see a God deeply concerned with our lives on earth and even more so concerned with our eternal destination. Somehow, Jesus manages to address them both seamlessly.

If we take the time to read chapters 8 and 9 of Matthew's Gospel, we will see Jesus on a tear healing people physically. He cures a leper (Matthew 8:1-4), a centurion's paralyzed servant (Matthew 8:13), Peter's mother-in-law who was lying in bed with a fever (Matthew 8:14-15), many possessed by demons, and many who were sick (Matthew 8:16-17); He heals two Gaderene demoniacs (Matthew 8:28-34), literally casting their demons into a herd of swine, a paralytic man (Matthew 9:1-8), a woman suffering from hemorrhages for twelve years (Matthew 9:18-26) , raises an official's daughter from death (Matthew 9:18-26), heals two blind men (Matthew 9:27-31), and heals a mute man (Matthew 9: 32-34). Then Matthew 9: 35-36 declares that Jesus "went around to all the towns and villages, teaching in the synagogues, proclaiming the Gospel of the kingdom, and curing every disease and illness" and that his heart was "moved with pity" for the crowds because they were "troubled and abandoned" and "like sheep without a shepherd."

This is Jesus. This is the heart of Jesus, God in the flesh who is massively concerned for us and wildly in love with us. He is a God who is not far from us and who holds nothing back to heal us. He is not far off, and He is not waiting for us to ascend to Him with our own human abilities. On the contrary, He knows of our human limitations and sinfulness, thus He became equal to us in His taking on flesh.

He then turns to His disciples who had witnessed all of these healings and miracles and invites them to do the same as He proclaims "the harvest is abundant, but the laborers are few, so ask the master of the harvest to send out more laborers for his harvest" (Matthew 9:37-38). And then we see Jesus drive home His desire for us as He sends His disciples out into the world to proclaim His kingdom in the very next chapter (Matthew 10:1-15). Jesus gives them all authority over unclean spirits and commands them to drive out sickness and unclean spirits. He concludes His mandate to them in Matthew 10: 6-8 as He orders them "go rather to the lost sheep of the house of Israel. As you go make this proclamation The kingdom of heaven is at hand. Cure the sick, raise the dead, cleanse lepers, drive out demons. Without cost you have received, without cost you are to give."

This is the heart of Christ. It is one amazing thing to read of God curing someone in great need, but it is far more amazing to see God ordering us to go and do the same. This speaks volumes of who Jesus is; it portrays His character as an all loving and holy God. There is no other name above the name of Jesus.

Deathbed Questions

So now we find ourselves back sitting at the foot of the bed of my friend Basri. Withered away skin clinging to frail bones, isolated in his dark and lonely bedroom. Absolutely unable to perform any work or saving act on his own. Lost in his sadness and sin, unable to bridge the sinful gap between himself and God. Is it important for Basri to hear the Gospel of Jesus Christ? And does Jesus have anything to offer my friend, Basri? Is Jesus longing to comfort Basri?

I imagine Basri to be a character jumping right off the pages of Matthew 8 and 9. Quite honestly, he may be the most lost and forsaken, broken, and helpless person I have ever met. He literally cannot do anything on his own. I often ask myself, *if he were your son, or friend, or father, wouldn't you want to drag him to the feet of Jesus?* He is a man who is no doubt tormented by his life's choices. He is a man who has no doubt spent a lifetime walking away from Jesus. Yet here Jesus is, still pursuing His beloved until death.

Basri desperately needs to hear the Gospel of Jesus Christ, a Gospel of repentance, forgiveness, truth, love, and mercy. Basri needs physical healing, and even more, he needs forgiveness and spiritual awakening that only God can grant to him. His caretakers can come into his room each day and dress and bandage his physical wounds, and he can receive medication each day to fend off some of the gruesome symptoms of his horrid disease. But only Jesus can stop the bleeding in his soul; only Jesus can wipe away the years of sin and wrath within his soul. Only Jesus can save him.

One of Basri's great misfortunes is that he is a Muslim living in a Muslim country. And like all Muslims in this country, the government has strict laws about anyone proclaiming the Gospel to him. So Basri is physically restricted to his bed and spiritually restricted as he currently has very limited access to the Gospel of Jesus Christ. After a few months of getting to know him, I could just sense and feel the pain and longing in his eyes. He was so broken. I imagine that someone who has spent the majority of his life in destruction and is now bedridden has plenty of time to reflect upon his past miseries.

My heart aches deeply for my friend, and sometimes I often find myself longing to share the love of Jesus with him. I long to tell him that with Jesus, his hope can be eternal and that with Jesus, this horrendous existence of his final days can be turned into an eternal and joyful celebration. There is hope with Jesus.

Each day we visit with him, I discover new and creative ways the Holy Spirit is showing me to share the Gospel of Jesus with him. It has been amazing to see how God is madly in love with Basri and has not yet given up on him. Basri now clearly knows that Jesus is pursuing him.

I shudder to imagine myself lying on my deathbed in spiritual torment like that, and but for the grace of God, you and I will be one day. At that point in life, nothing we can do or have done will be able to bring us to God our Father in heaven. Many of the religions of the world teach us that God is a grand mountain to be ascended, and that if we work and climb hard enough, we can be with Him forever.

But what about Basri? What about all men and women like him who have little to no physical and mental ability to climb anything? What about you and me? Apart from God coming down to me in grand pursuit of rescue, I will never reach eternity. I am dead on my own each and every day; yet sadly, it often takes an image of a broken, crippled man to remind me of my desperation.

Yet there is such great, beautiful, and enormous hope in one name: the name of Jesus! For God so loved the world he sent his one and only son so that whosoever believes in him shall not perish but have everlasting life" (John 3:16).

Chapter 9: It Takes Families

"The future of evangelization depends in great part on the Church of the home."[26]

– Saint Pope John Paul II

We could sense every eye upon us as we journeyed through the community pool. All eight of us . . . Lacy and I and our six kids were most likely the only Christians in the park that day. Most of the Muslim families there had most likely never seen a family like ours.

Far too often we have settled and resigned as a young family into the comfort of our home. We have said things like, *surely we can't take all the kids with us there?* Or, *maybe we can serve in that capacity once the kids are older?* So instead, we focus more on our careers, our children's educations, and our retirement accounts, inevitably reducing our Church participation, by and large, to a one-hour Sunday experience. And as a father of six, believe me, I understand that even that obligation can feel like running a marathon at times.

A Light To The Entire World

Perhaps you are reading this book and you are married or have a family; you most likely are asking yourself, *but how can I be a light to the world when I have so many responsibilities and worries with my own family?* I doubt you are alone in your questioning.

Jesus tells us that we are to be salt and light in a bland and darkened world (Matthew 5:13-16). But how can my family be Christ's light to the world if we focus only on ourselves and fearfully become a family in hiding? I see it everywhere, starting with me. It's just far easier to not be involved when you have newborns and toddlers climbing all over the place, screaming, peeing, and spitting on everyone. But for some reason, Jesus tells us that the kingdom of heaven belongs to these children (Luke 18:16). He tells us that we must become little children in order to receive Him (Matthew 18:3). So according to Jesus, it sounds like the world needs our children. The world needs our loud, messy, and dirty kids. And who are we to hoard them to ourselves against the will of God?

In our experience, being a family of eight in foreign missions has given us more opportunity to share the Gospel than we ever dreamed of. It is God's design for the family to mirror the very essence of God. Big families, small families, families without kids, and families with children. Every opportunity, from walking through the airport as a family to having my children lay hands upon the lost, poor, and sick in prayer, has been prepared for us by the Holy Spirit who is the principal agent of mission.[27]

I'll never forget when we brought Andrew back into our small rural town in Coopevega. Many people back home questioned if having our newborn baby in this rural Central American village was a good and safe thing to do. What about the mosquitoes and holes in the walls of your small, sweltering hot house? Will he sleep under a bug net, too? What about dengue? Do people over there vaccinate?

On our first week back home in Coopevega, we visited our dear friends Felipe and Rosario, who lived in destitute poverty. Flies and bugs everywhere, poor to nonexistent plumbing, you name the setback, they lived in it. When we walked into their small home, the heat and smell were smothering, but more smothering was the love in the room.

This family had longed to see our new gift from God; they couldn't hold in their joy and excitement. They had seen us and come to know us so well during the time Lacy was pregnant. They had come to know this crazy family who had moved countries away to serve them and to share the Gospel with them. They had fallen in love with Andrew long before he was even born. Andrew was their child as well; their joy was now overflowing.

To be honest, Lacy and I were both hesitant and somewhat skeptical if we should allow them to hold Andrew at first. I'm embarrassed to write that. After all, one of them could not even get up to walk much less wash her hands. We feared she could pass something on to him. All of our other five kids were born in America, and before anyone was allowed to hold them, the understanding was generally that you go and wash your hands or put some hand sanitizer on.

But here we were, in the middle of the jungle, so to speak. With joy and expectation, she plunged for her Andrew, taking him from our hands. She quickly eliminated that decision away from us. I had never seen someone so welcoming of a newborn baby. She cried tears of joy and her warm and soft hands (cleansed by God alone) held our new infant child with all the love, care, and protection of God the Father.

Her joy was uncontrollable. She laughed and cried some more. I'm certain her tears of joy dripped onto our Andrew. In Spanish, she announced what a gift from God our sweet baby boy was. Her spirit was lifted, and suddenly, Lacy and I had no concern about her sanitation. She needed Andrew, and we needed to witness her joy and awe. Andrew was carefully passed around by everyone in that house that day. His soft skin and the new baby smell was enough to bless anyone within a great distance.

Andrew is still being passed around to this day. He is now nearing two years old, and I am fairly certain that he is the best evangelizer of our family. Because we have moved to Asia, he has traded Spanish for Mandarin or Bahasa and Thai, but he is still the same bright light to the world. He is no stranger to a Hindu, Muslim, or a Buddhist; he joyfully welcomes them all in the same loving manner. He sees no distinction of race or creed. His smile breaks down walls, his wandering curiosity allows others to ponder the depths of God, and he and his five siblings completely disarm anyone who speculates or doubts our motive of love.

Our Family Missions Company founders, Frank and Genie Summers, have long stated "children make the best missionaries," and I couldn't agree with them more. Our Church has volumes of teaching and instruction on marriage and family, yet so many people in the world rarely see our teaching on marriage and family in action. We can spend hours and hundreds of words on social media telling people how great our understanding and teaching on marriage and family is, yet still people often fail to embrace it. I have discovered that our families are the means to place the Church's teaching on marriage and family into reality and perspective. We are the mantle to display her years of wisdom and teaching, even amid our brokenness.

I notice almost every time I am out and about here in a Muslim country alone, the general perception of me is far different than when I am with my wife and children. When I am alone, I sense that people tend to just glance at me in quick speculation: *Is he a tourist? Is he here making money?* For the most part, no one feels comfortable to walk up to me and strike up a conversation. And if they do, I find that it tends to land on the topics of American politics or what's happening in America at that time. All very surface-level things.

But when I am out and about with my wife and children, I am always amazed at how many smiles we receive. Like, huge, big, staring type smiles as if people were looking at something beautiful and amazing on display before them. People will stop what they are doing and walk up to us. We even have employees at stores and food stalls stop what they are doing and pick up our children. And the conversations generally tend to have comments like: *How beautiful your children are! Oh wow, what a great, big family you have!*

Just stop a moment and think about the differences between those two encounters. One is a super-surface-level conversation, and the other we are talking about the very attributes of God: truth, beauty, love . . . The second allows me to declare with great humility but with great confidence, "Yes! Children are indeed a blessing! A true gift from our God who is madly in love with us." Instantly those walls are broken down.

Instead of some foreign tourist, I am given certain credibility. All because of my children and wife; all because I am part of a family. A family intact and on display, even with all its shortcomings, is a witness to the world that God is love. When people see our families, they have the opportunity to behold God. Don't sell yourself or God short on this truth; families can evangelize the world. We see it happen nearly every day.

From the Eyes and Mouths and Hands of Babes

Just the other day, all eight of us returned home to our apartment and encountered our dear friend Auntie Kris. Auntie Kris is a beautiful Hindu woman who works the front gate of our apartment. She sees us come and go all the time. She often laughs at us as all eight of us cram into one taxi.

She screams to us, “Jalan! Jalan!” which means *street, street* literally . . . She is basically saying, *there you all go again, always on the street!*

Each day when we leave, we make sure to stop and talk to her, get to know her, and just love on her. She holds Andrew, and the girls always tend to run up to her in joy as if she is an aunt to them. As we returned home, we asked her how she was doing like most days. On this day, she complained of both her feet being in great pain and a terrible swelling of her feet. She went on and on explaining her pain, and indeed as we glanced at her bare feet, we could see the immense swelling.

It's amazing because our children already knew what we were going to do; they had already gathered around her. We asked her if we could pray for her and ask Jesus to relieve her pain and heal her feet. She smiled and agreed.

As a family, we all laid our hands on her warm, swollen feet. Even Andrew's one-year-old fingers touched her pain laden and tired feet. We called upon the name of Jesus and the power of the Holy Spirit to heal and comfort her at that very moment. We prayed with faith that Jesus was able to heal and comfort her, and she witnessed that. The rest was up to God.

Our children have witnessed great and incredible things, and they have even been a part of great and incredible miracles. We try our best to bring them into our mission daily; sometimes they lead the way, and we follow.

But How?

So many people assume that to be a missionary disciple of Jesus, you have to be able to raise people from the dead, turn water into wine, or walk on water. Let me assure you that no one in our family can do any of those things, although we are holding out hope with Andrew, as he is only one and a half years old. Time will tell.

To be a missionary disciple of Jesus Christ simply means that we are willing and able to use the gifts given to us by God in baptism and confirmation. Radically and generously, not sparingly. And none of my children are even confirmed yet, so apparently, baptism gets us pretty far down the road. So ask yourself a simple question, "Am I baptized and in love with Jesus Christ?" If so, then you are ready to go. We just have to be willing and available. That's the deal.

Often in my life, I am not willing and available. I may often be willing and available to put in extra time at work or school or in a relationship. I may be willing and available to make time for an annual vacation or a night out with friends, and those things are great. But to be a disciple of Jesus Christ, I have to be intentional. It doesn't just happen by accident. But there is absolutely no secret ingredient other than being open to the Holy Spirit using us. But I will warn you, it takes our time and often will change our plans, and that is where the challenge lies. But other than that, it can be so extremely fundamental.

For example, as I have mentioned earlier, here in Asia, at least once per week, we visit a home for extremely sick and dying AIDS patients. Because it is a Muslim country, we are forbidden to preach or really even speak about Jesus to them. Most of what we do is simply show up and visit with these lost, hurt, abandoned, and dying, beautiful people. Essentially anyone with love in their hearts can do it. And we have yet to show up and see a line of people waiting to visit them. They are so lost, hurt, and abandoned.

We received no extensive training to serve them, and we possess no specific medical skill set either. But what we do have to offer them is our time and our hearts. Our time is theirs for that hour and a half. No phones, no distractions. We have no other plans, just to be present to them. And our hearts are always overflowing with love for them. Our smiles and laughter can be contagious, and our family dynamic is on display, and they know we are Christians.

After a couple of visits, they knew that the only reason we were there was to love them. Eventually, we were able to pray with the patients who were Christians as allowed by law, and so many walls were broken down over time. Our children made them beautiful drawings with hearts and crosses on them, handed out candy and crafts to them. They knew that the love of Christ compelled us into their home. Now when we go there, some of them expect us to pray for them, as they have grown accustomed to it.

We are a family on a mission for this little small and forgotten community of forgotten people in the eyes of society. I can guarantee you we aren't anything special, and we don't do anything phenomenal when we show up. We just give them our time and hearts. We have even been able to share the Gospel with some of them who aren't Christian. Is that not what Jesus calls forth from us in the greatest commandment: "You shall love the Lord, your God, with all your heart, with all your soul, and with all your mind and you shall love your neighbor as yourself" (Matthew 22: 37,39). Sure, I as a forty-year-old man may be called to proclaim the Word of God in preaching or in writing, but as a family, our mere presence often speaks louder than any talk I could give or any teaching on the Trinity that I could share with them.

I could go on and on about how our family has been a witness, and most of it is in ways we never planned or set out to do because the Holy Spirit is in charge. I've witnessed some of the hardest of hearts and some of the most drug- and alcohol-addicted men stop dead in their tracks and ponder the beauty and godliness of our family, and please understand me when I say we are not always a graceful sight to behold. We often fight, scream, and get angry with one another. But that's just part of life.

Just the other day, we were on a train ride from one Asian country into another, and our whole family was sitting down taking up four benches on the hot and rundown train. I noticed an elderly man kept glancing over at us, and eventually, his glancing turned into full-fledged staring. Sometimes we can be quite the spectacle. His interest turned into him asking me about all my children. With one daughter on my lap and another leaning over my shoulder, I began to ask him about his life.

He told me he was a Chinese Freethinker who had five different wives, and that he has a total of seven children with all his wives. He said he didn't believe in God, and that he assumed his being a good person would merit him any type of eternal life should such a crazy thing as that exist. I could just sense the desire for something (someone) deeper in his eyes as he spoke with me.

With several of my children hanging onto me, I was able to share the Gospel with him. Really dig down deep and share the entire thing with him. Our train ride ended and we parted ways, but our family continues to pray for that man. The thing that amazes me so much about this encounter and many others like it is that without my children scattered everywhere on that train, I don't think he and I would have had such a deep and meaningful conversation. It's almost as if God used and honored our beautiful children to soften this man's heart and to open his ears to the words God had to share with him. The kingdom of God does indeed belong to children; it's almost as if they are the gatekeepers, opening the doors wide for all the world to see the love of God the Father.

The world is waiting for our families to come out of hiding, to come out of our routines and plans, and declare the goodness and beauty of the risen Jesus. A Jesus that can take back what the enemy has stolen from them. One day when we get to heaven, I can't wait to see the many healings, conversions, and changes the little hands and prayers of my children have done in the kingdom of God. I am certain it will be overwhelming.

Just the other day, as we were leaving our apartment, Auntie Kris was all smiles as usual.

"My feet feel so much better!" she exclaimed with great joy.

My little six-year-old Norah tucked her grin in a bit and looking up she smiled at me as if to say, *Look, Dad, our prayers really worked. Jesus healed her.* When we tell our children that God can work miracles, they often will shrug us off. But when we invite them into working miracles through the power of the Holy Spirit, they will never forget it; it becomes so real to them. They will see their faith in Jesus as something real and something worthy to give up the rest of their lives for.

Unintended Blessings

When we lived in Costa Rica, one of my favorite things to do was drive across the country from our home to the airport. In about five hours, we could encounter rural, dirt, and dusty roads so rundown you would wonder if you were lost; majestic sunrises over volcanoes and waterfall filled mountains flourishing with monkeys, sloths, and colors of birds I didn't even know existed. When our air conditioning went out for good in the van, we were forced to open the windows and let the best of Costa Rica in. Driving was often majestic. But perhaps my favorite thing about these trips was stopping along the way to smell the roses, or as my kids and wife might say "Dad stopping along the way to buy every type of fruit and food offered in the street."

I was and will always be a roadside food and drink junkie. Whether it was roadside smoked meats or the juiciest mangoes known to man, I always found it hard to stay on the road in Costa

Rica and just drive. My favorite stop was a young twenty-something-year-old who would sell the most delicious ice-cold, fresh-squeezed orange juice. He was located along a pretty busy highway, but we could pull the van over and he would run up to the car and hand you the large cups of fresh, delicious, ice-cold orange juice and a fresh bag of oranges from his grove. It was amazing. The first time I stopped, it was just William and me on a little trip, and it was so good that after that, rarely did we ever pass by and not stop to indulge.

When we began as foreign missionaries, I think I tended to focus on the things I was going to have to do away with; we had so much to get rid of and walk away from. At times, I found myself counting the cost to become foreign missionaries. We lost money, property, businesses, and most importantly, a life that included such proximity to an amazing family and amazing friends. On some days of doubt, I felt like we were shooting ourselves in the foot.

But as we progressed on our journey, God showed us so many little unintended blessings of serving Him. Like ice-cold orange juice on the side of the road in 100-degree weather. It seems He is always blessing us with more. Here in Asia, we have tasted such an exotic cuisine ranging from rich and spicy Indian curries to delicious Chinese and Malaysian noodles for breakfast. In Costa Rica, we had people constantly knocking on our doors selling fresh bread, *momonchinos* just picked off the tree, and juicy pineapples. William and I discovered the most epic natural waterfall into a nearby river one day, and I will never forget the sound of his joy-filled screaming as he barreled down it with such enthusiasm.

"Holy cow, Dad! You go next! It's so awesome!"

We have seen beaches and volcanoes, beautiful temples, and all ridden in tuk-tuks only designed to fit four people. We have been exposed to cultural treasures that are often hidden away from us in the West. Our children have been forced to learn new languages and understand people from different nations. Our kids have had their faith tested as they have been asked to pray over people for miracles at a moment's notice. Our lives are overflowing with what Lacy and I refer to as unintended blessings of serving as missionary disciples. These are blessings we believe God has given to us because He loves us and constantly longs to remind us of His nearness. These are blessings we know that would have been hidden from us had we never had left the comfort and ease of our life before missions.

Now Is the Time

"I tell you, brothers, the time is running out . . ."

– 1 Corinthians 7:29

The Holy Spirit is waiting, longing to use our families to evangelize a lost and broken world if only we would have the courage and humility to step out in faith. And while the Holy Spirit is longing to use us, the world is longing to hear the goodness and truth of the Gospel of Jesus. Indeed, "the harvest is abundant, but the laborers are few" (Luke 10:2), so let us, as Christ says, ask the Lord of the harvest for more laborers. Let us also be not afraid to become the laborers Christ is calling forth from among us. Close to three billion people in the eastern hemisphere have never heard of Jesus. Wow! Millions of people in the Americas need a deep re-evangelization.

I believe Saint John Paul the Great is spot on, and yes, "the future of evangelization will depend in great part on the Church of the home." So now is the time for us as families to abandon our fears, and even our dreams, and take Christ to the world *as a family*. Don't waste your twenties, thirties, forties, and fifties pursuing riches that do not matter in the eyes of God; rather let us be like the man in Matthew 13:44, who found a treasure in a field and joyfully sold all he had for that one single treasure. I am finding that serving Christ and presenting Him as our treasure to a lost and broken world is far richer in the eyes of God. Taking Christ as our treasure is how we become salt and light in the world.

Soon (enough), our children will all be grown and out of the house . . . We will have a new array of alluring temptations to buckle us down and stay in the house. We will be "too old" for that ministry, and we will have lost a step or two. Now is the time, and our families are the means that Christ will use to present His Gospel. A Gospel that changes lives. Come, Holy Spirit.

Chapter 10: Risk

"Teach us to give and not count the cost."[28]

– St. Ignatius of Loyola

"I told the bishop that if I am ever thrown into prison, not to come and bail me out, just take care of my family. But I will not pass on the opportunity to share the Gospel with a Muslim in need." Deacon Albert has now become a great friend of ours, and these were some of the first words he spoke to me regarding living and serving in a Muslim country. His humility, zeal, and faithfulness are exactly what are needed to make disciples in a country that forbids you to speak to Muslims about Jesus.

For so much of the world, it is an enormous and risky task to profess Christ as your Lord and King, and to attempt to follow Him daily. It was very hard for me to fathom this truth, and I even doubted the truth of it until I moved my family to serve in Asia. It is just a different reality in much of the world than I have grown up with living in North America.

To profess Christ as King is a risky business, but this is nothing new. Jesus speaks about risk in the scriptures, but He constantly assures us that His providence will always sustain us. "They will seize you and persecute you, they will hand you over to the synagogues, and to prisons, and they will have you led before governors because of my name" (Luke 21:12), and "You will be hated by all because of my name, *but not a hair on your head will be destroyed*" (Luke 21:18).

We have a friend here in Asia who fled from Pakistan for her safety. "Oh, they sometimes burn the Christians where I am from," she exclaimed to me as we were in a Church honoring a set of Asian relics. This is real-life risk, and it exists in a real way in real-time in much of the world.

These are some of the headlines I have read in just the last year of my life:

"25 Christians Killed In Nigeria by Boko Haram"

"Boko Haram Destroys Christian Village and Church in Africa"

"Nigerian Mass Becomes a Massacre"

"Mass Grave of Christians Killed by Islamic State Found in Syria"

"Gunmen in Egypt Attack Bus Carrying Christians"

"Sri Lanka Church and Hotel Bombings Kill 258 People"

Although the list goes on and on, I will stop there because there is no need to grant any more recognition to these horrible acts of evil than has already been granted to them. But the truth is evident; it is extremely risky to be a Christian in a large part of the world today.

Love Conquers All

If there is one abounding truth in all of Christianity for us to truly lay our head upon it is the truth that God is love and His love has and will continue to conquer all evil in the world.

So yes indeed, to follow Jesus is risky, but on the other hand, to follow Jesus is the only place I truly long to be. Even if he calls me to the most hardened, dark, and risky places on the globe. This past Easter morning, we returned to our apartment after Mass to read about the horrendous bombings that had occurred in nearby Sri

Lanka. My heart sunk, and I had a deep burning in my stomach; I was almost in tears.

Just a little less than a year ago, we were in discussions with a bishop and priest in Sri Lanka to move our family there to serve as missionaries. A flood of panic and *what-ifs* stormed through my mind, O*h, my God, what if we would have moved there? Would we all have been in one of those churches? Would we all have died? Would some of us have died? Would my children have had to live through that horrible experience and have seen some of their family members die in such a horrendous way?* Fear can be so crippling; it can grab us like a strong wave at sea and pull us completely under the waters of despair, holding us there for a terribly long time.

But I have realized that the Holy Spirit does not want me to live in fear, because remember that where the spirit of the Lord, is there is always freedom (2 Corinthians 3:17). He moves us into the depths of freedom and love. What if we would have been there? Well then God would have been right there with us as well. It's a risk we take as a result of being a Christian. But the truth is that even in death we cannot be separated from the love of God in Christ (Romans 8:38-39), and yes, though we may be "hated because of the name of Christ, not a single hair on our head will be destroyed" (Luke 21:18). Who else in the world can offer us this type of freedom and love?

St. Paul stated it best when he wrote "For me to live is Christ to die is gain" (Philippians 1:21) Even amid evil and potential death, we have nothing to fear because we have the love and mercy of Jesus Christ. Jesus reminds us of this Himself when He declares "do not be afraid of those who kill the body but cannot kill the soul; rather, be afraid of the one who can destroy both soul and body in Gehenna" (Matthew 10:28).

Some people ask me if I am crazy serving as a Catholic Missionary with my wife and children in a country which forbids me to do so, and quite honestly, I question my own sanity at times. But it is during these times of questioning that I recall such scriptures, and I am reminded that love conquers all. Love is the only answer to a world filled with hate. Fear is not the answer. For me to simply fold my faith and hope in Jesus inward and become a coward is not the answer. We have the answer, and His name is Jesus, and the world is in desperate need of Him and nothing else.

Abandoning the Trap of Safety

I have to admit to you that I am a big wimp. I'll go ahead and state my biggest fears to you, and those who are closest to me can attest. I am afraid of open saltwater, as in oceans filled with sharks and deep blue waters. My brother can tell you that even as a child, I wondered if there were sharks in every swimming pool we swam in growing up. I am afraid of needles and hate to get shots, or draw blood. You can ask my wife about that one. I am a wimp. In my life, I have avoided the dentist, doctors, and booster shots all because I hate needles. But as a Christian, I cannot go on living my life plagued by my fears; I can't just avoid all risk in fear of encountering it, especially if I am determined to share the Gospel with all nations.

One of my favorite quotes regarding risk is attributed to John A. Shedd, "A ship in harbor is safe, but that is not what ships were built for."[29] Far too often I feel like I am seeking safety instead of embracing risk. I feel like I am seeking my harbor, my place of refuge, my peace here on Earth. Can you relate? And sadly, we often witness a Gospel preached that declares that our peace here on Earth is truly all we have to seek when the pursuit of heavenly peace should be our ultimate aim. Now is the time for us to drift away from our harbors and out onto the risky waters, not worry about what is out there, because ultimately, Jesus is the one out there waiting to meet us.

Can you imagine being close enough to Jesus that in the middle of the night out at sea with Him, you trust that He is asking you to step out onto the raging waters and walk towards Him (Matthew 14:22-33)? Again, with my fear of deep water, just typing that makes my fingers start to sweat a bit. But like Peter, I believe that now is the time for me to abandon the comforts and safety of my harbors and jump boldly out onto the waters with Jesus (Matthew 14:30)! Why? Because that's where Jesus is, and that's where Jesus has always been.

Can you imagine Jesus just sitting in the comfort of his boat while it is safely docked with his apostles for the three years of his earthly ministry? Never really leaving the comforts of the harbor. No waves to encounter, no demons to expel, no Pharisees to encounter, no miracles to perform, not even one sinner to pursue and save. Or can you imagine the apostles just simply remaining in the upper room and never allowing the Holy Spirit to take them from nation to nation spreading the Gospel? The Church as we know it today wouldn't be in existence, and your faith and mine may not have been born.

So is the case today. I have to constantly be asking myself, *Lord, where? Where can I take a risk for your kingdom? Where do you want me to go with you today, Jesus? I'll go anywhere with you!* Because if I don't ask those questions prayerfully, I will remain in my harbor of safety with no miracles, no demons expelled, and no souls offered salvation. It's as simple as that. If we desire to take the Gospel to the ends of the earth as commanded by Christ, then we have to take risks, sometimes even great risks, like the apostles and great saints before us have done. The Gospel will not progress to the entire world with a Church content in the safety of a calm harbor.

Perhaps you and I will never come face to face with the horrors of persecution or martyrdom, and perhaps we will. Perhaps the rewards of our risk will look different than Saint Peter's did, and that's okay. But our risk is worth it, because Jesus is worth it, and because Jesus is with us in our risk. He is out on the water waiting and beckoning us in.

Helping Others Jump

Once while attending a men's retreat the facilitator invited us out onto a boat as the sun was setting. The retreat was coming to an end, and we were watching a beautiful sunset. Day turned into night, and the facilitator was calling us deeper into the heart of Christ; he was calling us to go deeper with Jesus in our lives. He finished his talk and he declared loudly to all of us that he was going all-in with Jesus; he was going deeper. After saying this, he stood on the front of the boat and plunged himself into the water fearlessly.

Instantly, a shot of passion and adrenaline jolted through me. I stood up, and I knew I had to jump into the water. Jumping into the water for me represented an expression of freedom and a willingness to walk closer with Christ, to take a risk with Him. Sometimes we just have to take a risk and, like Peter, just go meet Jesus out on the waters of risk. He will never abandon us or fail us when we do so.

As our retreat leader plunged out, apparently I wasn't the only one with a jolt of energy. Everyone in the boat cleared out and jumped into the waters. So his taking a risk by jumping into the waters inspired us all to take a risk and go deeper.

Remember, nothing happens with a ship in a harbor; it's simply resting there and preparing to be sent back out into the deep and risky waters. Look around yourself and see what the people you surround yourself with are doing. Are they ships safely docked at the harbor for their entire lives, or are they ships willingly moving back out onto the deep and risky waters with Christ? Look at your weekly or monthly Bible Study, is anyone jumping out onto the water with Jesus, or is everyone just sitting around comfortably?

I fear that too much of my life has been and will be spent docked safely in a harbor, and I can't stand the thought of that. Don't be fooled that the harbor is the best place for you to spend your life, even if everyone around you is docked there.

Here Is My Life, Lord

If you are anything like me, then now and then you notice how time is zipping by at an uncontrollable rate. Very soon, it will all be over for you and me, and I don't want to examine my life and realize that I was a ship who rarely departed from the harbor. There have been so many incredible risk takers before us in the Church, and their legacies constantly beckon me to go deeper, deeper into the will of Jesus Christ

Consider Saint Mother Teresa of Calcutta, who risked her life each day as she humbly knelt before dying lepers and infected AIDS patients, lovingly washing and dressing their wounds. Or what about St. Patrick, who so bravely responded to a vision from God to return to Ireland, a place where he had been enslaved years before, and spread the good news of the Gospel? As I have continued to grow in my Catholic faith, I believe God is calling me to view the lives of the saints before us as men and women who are inviting us deeper into the heart of Jesus instead of viewing them as some sort of Catholic Superhero. I truly believe we all possess what they had. It's hidden in there deep within our core; sometimes I may just have to dig deeper and dig out a bunch of garbage around it and take a risk.

Chapter 11: Suffering As Currency

"These last few days I've spent many wakeful nights trembling thinking of the task I now begin—that of eulogizing my own precious child.

"How does one do this? How do you sum up the sublime devotion, the exquisite innocence, or the tender affections and pangs of sorrow, in short how do you sum up a person's life in a mere speech of words bedewed with tears of paternal affection? You don't."[30]

– Jonathan Kiehl

These were the words of a dear friend of mine, Jonathan Kiehl, as he began to tearfully yet prophetically eulogize his very own son, Ezekiel. Beautiful Ezekiel was born in the humble mission fields of Mexico as his parents had recently sold all they owned and completely given their lives to Christ and His Church as Catholic Missionaries. Less than two years later, Ezekiel would die in his father's consoling arms in those same humble mission fields of Mexico.

As a parent of six children of my own, I can barely bear the thought of even imagining what my dear friends went through in the days, months, and years following Ezekiel's death, and I can't even imagine the pain and suffering they still endure today because of this great loss. Just imagine for a moment being forced to bury your own child, the one you loved and cared for so dearly, the one who was still stealing your heart with such innocence and grace each day. I imagine his sweet smile melted their hearts and brightened even the darkest of their days. "The Lord gave and the Lord has taken away, blessed be the name of the Lord" (Job 1:21).

When I reflect upon my friends losing their child so dramatically, he drowned in a small pool in their Mexican town, I can't help but ponder the sharp words of St. Theresa of Avila when she declared to Jesus, "If this is how you treat your friends, it is no wonder you have so few!"[31]

All That Glitters

When I was in my early twenties and sincerely beginning to live for Jesus, I used to look around at Christians a bit older than me and just imagine how incredibly perfect their lives must be. They were young and vibrant, dressed better than me, newly married and having kids, coming into their own in their careers, buying new cars and homes. Most of them seemed to have placed most of their rough and troubled times behind them. Some of them would share testimonies of how God was blessing them with so much here on Earth. I think I became enamored with a sense of glitter surrounding their lives. It wasn't that they were stating that their lives were perfect; it just seemed that their life with Christ was lacking in any pain and suffering. I believe I internalized what I witnessed with a simple thought, *Wow! If I follow Jesus, I can have this great life without problems as well.*

I figure it's somewhat of a natural human tendency to think this way, and perhaps I am not alone in doing this? I almost can sense that in the Church, we can paint a picture that to follow Jesus is to receive a better life here on Earth, one with fewer problems and one with more security. I must confess that I believed that while I was younger, I even expressed this to other people. It was portrayed in the following subtle yet real expressions, "Just give up your sins to follow Jesus. He will give you such a better life. A life with meaning and purpose." While there is absolutely nothing wrong with that expression, I think it is what I did *not* mention and still sometimes fail to mention that can lead some people astray when it comes to following Jesus.

To follow Jesus is to die, and to die on this Earth is to suffer, and that can sting. Dietrich Bonhoeffer, the German pastor and theologian who was hanged in a Nazi concentration camp, stated it as such, "When Christ calls a man, He bids him come and die."[32] Bonhoeffer is essentially paraphrasing the words of Jesus Christ Himself. "Whoever wishes to come after me must deny himself, take up his cross, and follow me. For whoever wishes to save his life will lose it, but whoever loses his life for my sake will find it" (Matthew 16:24).

Our founder at Family Missions Company, Genie Summers, always proclaims with such humility yet certitude, "Suffering is the currency of the Kingdom of God!" For me that can be an immensely challenging statement to believe and accept, yet I know it is Gospel truth and I have seen its truth lived out throughout the life of our beautiful Church. Not too many of the saints had a shiny and glittery life. As I have slowly come to study many of their lives, I can see so many common themes among them, and the primary theme is a life of suffering.

The great saints have suffered alongside Christ, and suffered with Him much. Think of the apostles of Jesus Christ being martyred, St. Maximillian Kolbe in a gas chamber, St. Mother Teresa of Calcutta slum dwelling, and St. Laurence being martyred on an open fire, just to start. Deep down within me, I truly want to follow Jesus like these men and women have, yet at the same time, I carry so much resistance to suffering with Christ. Sometimes I prefer to think of life with Christ as some polished up, refined, and wide road.

Stadiums of Christians

When I was a teenager, I attended this great enormous Catholic Conference in a stadium. The weekend event proved to be a life changing event for me, as the graces of the Holy Spirit seemed to awaken the gifts and fruits of the Holy Spirit already placed within me through Baptism and Confirmation. Most of us reading this book are no stranger to such an event like a stadium gathering for Christ. The late and great Billy Graham revolutionized the stadium movement with his fruitful Promise Keepers campaign, and every Christian denomination seems to have some such movement within its life and body. They can be glorious occasions.

I wish all of us believers in Christ, whether Catholic, Protestant, or anything in between, could all be gathered into a stadium for one weekend together. But we could sort of flip the script, and instead of inspiring talks about what God has to offer us to improve ourselves, I wish we could behold the generous invitation He has for us to suffer alongside Him.

We could focus on the initial invitation of Christ to us all to "lose our lives" (Matthew 8: 34-36). We could show videos of the trials and tribulations of St. Paul out on the mission fields (2 Corinthians 11:22-29), the martyrdom of many of the apostles, and the current persecutions thousands of Christians are receiving today in Asia, Africa, or the Middle East. While I know and understand that this event would not sell out or even draw many attendees, I do feel like it may be a more honest presentation of what it means to follow Jesus. It is not a wide road at all.

At the end of our event, as the videos and talks are concluded, we could have our giant altar call.

Anyone who now still wants to follow Jesus can come forward. You may lose your home or son or daughter. You may be deeply misunderstood and persecuted for the sake of righteousness. Jesus may ask you to give up your lucrative career or break up with your girlfriend. Your life may end in horrible martyrdom, or you may even be imprisoned for your faith in Jesus. You will be sent as sheep among wolves (Matthew 10:16). Now, who would like to come down? Just walk up to the front please.

I honestly have to ask myself the following questions: *Would I step forward and walk to the front of the stadium? Am I only following Jesus because I can gain a better life here on Earth? Would I follow Jesus if I knew my life would end like one of the apostles?*

These are tough questions for me to wrestle with, but if I am to follow Jesus as his disciple, no matter how great the temptation is, I can't assume that I can circumvent suffering. What St. Paul declares in the letter to the Philippians has to well up within me like a great fountain of joy, "For to you has been granted, for the sake of Christ, not only to believe in Him, but also to suffer for Him" (Phil 1:29).

Acquiring Great Amounts of Currency

When we lived in Costa Rica, one of the most glorious sounds to our family—in fact, it was music to our ears—was the sound of air blowing through the pipes of our kitchen sink. I'll explain. You see, our small town was indeed blessed to have drinkable water, but often, it would just give out at various times throughout the day. This was new and challenging for our family. We often had no clue when it would happen, so sometimes we were caught off guard. We may have had a sink full of dirty dishes or no water stored up to drink or shower, and sometimes it would just go out. We always left the kitchen sink valve open so that when the water supply came back on, we could hear it and know. It would make a loud hissing sound which was caused by the air pressure pushing the water back into our pipes.

"Agua, agua! Thank you, Jesus!" we would all belt out as it came rushing back out of the sink.

This was a minor occurrence of suffering for us, as we never really went more than five to ten hours without water, and generally, we could store some up so as not to be caught with no water at all. Sometimes William and I had to drive over to our friend's house, who had a small private water well, and we would fill up large coolers of water for the day or night. But this small occurrence of suffering also came with the offer of so much grace and a deeper dependency on God.

I'll never forget one day when the water went out and our girls were planning to make some lemonade with the fresh lemons that were given to us by a neighbor. Their excitement came to a halt when they realized that the water went out. Almost without thinking about it, my sweet little girls extended their hands and prayed over the kitchen sink, "Please, Jesus, give us some water so we can make some delicious lemonade!" In an instant our little girls were acquiring the currency of the kingdom; they were learning that their God was in control of everything, and that He had instilled in them a faith that could move mountains (Mark 11:22-24), and even repair a failing water system.

While the water didn't turn back on immediately, in about another hour or so, it came hissing back on loudly, and ecstatic five-year-old rejoicing broke out. They were now rejoicing in God's provision, and they were now so thankful for the simple, yet often taken for granted, running water supply. They were becoming rich in the kingdom of God because their suffering produced patience, faithfulness, and thanksgiving.

Suffering with Christ, no matter how small, produces faith and dependency on God; it strips us away from the notion that we are in control and always will be. Suffering reminds us that our God is greater than any affliction or setback we may have, and suffering is the school that teaches us to run to God when we cannot endure anymore. Suffering is indeed the currency of the Kingdom, and those who can attain this currency can receive true glory, as St. Paul states, "I consider that the sufferings of this present time are as nothing compared with the glory to be revealed for us" (Romans 8:18).

While we cannot earn our way into heaven by merely suffering, I have found in my life that no amount of suffering, big or small, has been unpaid by Jesus Christ. He honors our taking up our cross to follow Him, even our most broken and short-lived attempts.

We Suffer Because He First Suffered

"For this you have been called, because Christ also suffered for you, leaving you an example that you should follow in his footsteps."

– 1 Peter 2:21

It is so easy for me to try to avoid suffering at all costs, to take a wider road in reaching Jesus. It's so easy, yet such fool's gold. It seems like in our culture today many of us Christians (Catholic or non-Catholic) are selling a version of Christianity devoid of any type of suffering. The TV preacher has shiny white teeth, a bright dress or suit, and a new vacation or second home on the lake, all alluring us to get right with God and live our best life now like he is. It's like a subtle or not-so-subtle attempt to show us all the things Jesus can give us on Earth. I sort of cringe at times, and hope I am not giving off that same invitation. Sure, we have the freedom to pursue those things, but Jesus never promised them to us. Rather, Jesus guaranteed us suffering; "Remember the word I spoke to you, No slave is greater than his master. If they persecuted me, they will also persecute you" (John 15:20). And we are actually encouraged to rejoice when we experience suffering: "Beloved, do not be surprised that a trial by fire is occurring among you, as if something strange were happening to you. But, rejoice to the extent that you share in the sufferings of Christ, so that when his glory is revealed you may also rejoice exultantly" (1 Peter 4:12-13).

I'll never forget going to a Men's Night at a large Church in America one evening. The monthly event was catered with the most delicious food and drink; the seats were stuffed and comfy, and the room temperature just perfect. The pastor stood up at the front of the Church and welcomed all the men in, ensuring them that these Men's Nights at his Church were tailor made exactly for everyone there, and that all you had to do was just show up and be fed. He then rattled off a list of dynamic celebrity-type speakers his Church had lined up just for them that summer. Everything from professional athletes to popular musicians. It all just seemed so geared at appeasing and entertaining everyone.

I tried to imagine Jesus' Men's Nights while He walked the earth. His words were so tough and challenging and at times appalling for those around him to even listen to: "Amen, amen, I say to you, unless you eat the flesh of the Son of Man, and drink his blood, you do not have life within you" (John 6: 53); "No one who sets his hand to the plow and looks to what was left behind is fit for the kingdom of God" (Luke 9:62); and, "Not everyone who says Lord, Lord will enter the kingdom of heaven, but only the one who does the will of my father in heaven" (Matthew 7:21).

I don't claim to have all the answers to conducting Men's Nights, but I do know that the words of Jesus are terribly clear when it comes to genuinely following Him; we will indeed suffer. And we will suffer because He first suffered. Sometimes it's really as simple as that. His example was not ever one of prosperity alone and the avoidance of suffering. Even the one time in scripture when He seemed so overwhelmed by His suffering in the garden of Gethsemane, He turned to His Father and rededicated His willingness to suffer, crying out, "Take this cup from me, but not what I will, but what you will" (Mark 14:36).

While I am so far from the perfection of Christ, I am not called to be far off from His life of suffering. To suffer with Christ is to walk with Him and to be deeply united to Him. His invitation is indeed for us to come and die, but in that death, we have the invitation to receive so much life, glorious and eternal life.

I often think back to that Men's Night event and consider my own life and my own presentation of Jesus Christ and His Gospel in the world around me. When I present the Gospel to someone, what am I inviting them into? There is nothing wrong with inviting people to hear celebrity speakers or athletes, but as I read the words of Jesus in the Gospels, it seems clear to me that God is calling us deeper.

While I'm certain the pastor of that Church is a great and faith-filled man, at the end of the day, I don't even want to come close to presenting the Gospel of Jesus Christ as some wide road or comfortable place where I receive what I want, yet nothing is ever required of me. That's just not the Gospel. But there are many Christians who will present this type of prosperous life as the ultimate aim of the Gospel. Don't buy into that lie. Jesus' grand invitation to us is join Him in the ultimate mystery, that of suffering, dying, and rising with Him. His invitation stands anew each day, regardless of our failings or lack of faith. I long to have the humility and courage to offer my weaknesses to God and pray as St. Paul prayed:

> *"My grace is sufficient to you, for power is made perfect in weakness. I will rather boast most gladly in my weaknesses, in order that the power of Christ may*

dwell with me. Therefore, I am content with weaknesses, insults, hardships, persecutions, and constraints, for the sake of Christ, for when I am weak, then I am strong" (2 Corinthians 12:9-10).

Suffering Bears Fruit

My brave friends Johnathan and Theresa humbly eulogized their tender son before a Church filled with family and friends. They spoke of their son's love and their love for him. They spoke of the mission of their son's life, to bear witness to Jesus Christ, as they boldly declared, "Our son was born to be a missionary." As I reflect upon their tragic experience as parents, I can see the words of St. Paul come to life in dazzling form. "Now I rejoice in my sufferings for your sake, and in my flesh I am filling up what is lacking in the afflictions of Christ on behalf of His body, which is the Church" (Colossians 1:24).

It was almost as if my friends were rejoicing in the midst of their sufferings; they were finding a way to rejoice in the most devastating moment of their life. God's grace can accomplish amazing and impossible things through our suffering; it can present a clear picture of Jesus Christ and His glory and goodness. Grace can turn the greatest amount of sorrow into deep and lasting joy, and when we allow God to perform such a miracle through our own personal sufferings, the world around us will indeed look at Jesus Christ, the one who suffered so greatly for us, and declare that indeed there is nothing lacking in Him. Therefore, our suffering bears fruit in eternity because it is God who is now on display and not our devastation or sufferings. Now, every single time I encounter Jonathan and Theresa, I am reminded of their clear presentation of the Gospel: God is always present in suffering; God is always turning our suffering into the currency of His Kingdom.

Don't Trust Me, Trust Jesus

Sometimes I say too much, and I simply need to point to the words of Christ. If we truly long for blessing and favor with God, if we truly long for kingdom currency, we just need to listen to Christ and obey:

"When he saw the crowds, he went up to the mountain, and after he had sat down, his disciples came to him. He began to teach them, saying:

Blessed are the poor in spirit, for theirs is the kingdom of heaven.

Blessed are they who mourn, for they will be comforted.

Blessed are the meek, for they will inherit the land.

Blessed are they who hunger and thirst for righteousness, for they will be satisfied.

Blessed are the merciful, for they will be shown mercy.

Blessed are the clean of heart, for they will see God.

Blessed are the peacemakers, for they will be called children of God.

Blessed are they who are persecuted for the sake of righteousness, for theirs is the kingdom of heaven.

Blessed are you when they insult you and persecute you and utter every kind of evil against you falsely because of me. Rejoice and be glad, for your reward will be great in heaven. Thus, they persecuted the prophets who were before you."– Matthew 5:1-12

Part Two: Where Shall We Go?

Choose One or All and Go: The Lost, The Poor, and The Unreached

The world is constantly broadcasting to us what we should do with the rest of our lives, constantly suggesting where we should find our treasure and where we should exhaust the remaining energy of our lives.

I want my life to matter in the kingdom of God and in the life of others, and I don't want the rest of my days spent in selfish, indulgent living. Of the hundreds and thousands of pursuits presented to me in my short lifetime, I believe that the pursuit of the three categories below bring the most meaning to my life. I believe that if I exhaust my life on the three types of people below, I will more times than not find myself located in the center of God's will.

I generally cringe at placing people into categories, but for the sake of clarity in discovering the great treasure of taking Jesus Christ to the nations, perhaps we need a guideline or at least some directions along the way. My hope is that each of us can reflect upon these three groups of people, pray for the Holy Spirit to guide us to them, and then selflessly spend the rest of our lives among them, loving and serving them. All other pursuits in my life have seemed to pale greatly in light of pursuing the lost, poor, and unreached.

> <u>The Lost:</u> "I've never had an abortion, and this will be my first. I'm afraid, but the woman inside that building said everything will be okay. Tomorrow my problems will be gone."
>
> <u>The Poor:</u> "I don't have a mattress because they cost too much; I just sleep on the board with that blanket. If you have

an extra mattress, please give it to my wife; I'd say she needs it more than I do."

The Unreached: "I believe that when we light this incense each day the "god of guidance" will help us and grant guidance and prosperity in our lives."

Chapter 12: The Lost

"No one who meets Jesus ever stays the same."

– Philip Yancey

"I've never had an abortion, and this will be my first. I'm afraid, but the woman inside that building said if I have one, then everything will be okay, and tomorrow my problems will be gone."

These were the words a broken yet beautiful nineteen-year-old girl cried to me as I spoke with her outside an abortion clinic in America. My heart broke for her. Up to this point, much of my understanding of abortion was merely a far off concept. But now before me was this beautiful, young girl drowning in her pain. She didn't want to kill her baby, but clearly, she was in a jam, and she was looking for a way out. With tears in my eyes, I tried to smile, and I pleaded with her, asking her to give me a few minutes of her time.

I explained that I thought I could help her with her problem and perhaps I could find her some assistance, a home, and even some financial help to get her going as a young mom. I told her how beautiful her baby was inside her womb and that, although it was hard to believe me, she would eventually be an incredible mother.

For about twenty seconds, I could see a glimmer in her eye, a small voice of hope amid the voices of terror and despair that must have been replaying over and over in her head. Her wheels were spinning, and I could tell she was weighing my advice against the advice she received inside the clinic. She was hopeless. I gave her everything I had: phone numbers of care centers, shelters, prayer cards, my ear to listen, and even my phone number.

As she was weighing her options, an enraged female clinic employee barged outside the door and into the street between me and the girl. For a moment, I thought I was about to get hit. The woman was so uncomfortably close to me I could feel some of her sweat flying into my face.

"You get the hell out of here, sir! You don't care about these women! Not even one bit!" she screamed at me. Then some of the pro-life protesters started yelling out at the clinic worker. It became a bad scene. I remained calm as did the sweet young lady. I felt like I could see right through her eyes into her soul, and I knew she didn't want to kill her own child.

The little girl was so confused. She started to tear up. She was broken; she was lost. She drove off and returned a few hours later. She went through with the abortion, and I saw her leaving the facility later that day drenched in tears, holding onto her friend who had accompanied her. She was broken and gasping for life; this was the lowest moment of her nineteen years.

This sweet young girl is among the lost. She was tasting despair, what it is like to be separated from God. She had little to no hope; her joy had been trampled upon and stolen.

There are millions of people like her walking around us each day, trapped in a mental and spiritual prison, wondering how to be free. I have learned that if I sincerely open my heart, mind, and eyes, I can see them all around me daily. So many people around you and me are lost and wandering around in the darkness, and many of them will remain in this state for an entire lifetime.

The Church teaches us that "sin is present in human history; any attempt to ignore it or to give this dark reality other names would be futile" (CCC 386).[33] We live in a world of the lost. The lost are everywhere; not just inside of abortion clinics. The Lost are everyone from the single mom whose husband has just run off on her to the young boy pondering suicide because he feels he doesn't measure up to his friends. The Lost is the straight-A kid in school who is never enough for her parents, and the lost is the parent whose drive for a successful business has deprived them of anything else in life.

The Lost are different from both the poor and the unreached. The Lost can be every day going to school, working nine to five, or retired people. They aren't unreached because they have heard the Gospel and perhaps have grown up in a Christian environment, and they may or may not be materially poor. Quite simply, the lost are people around you and me who need Jesus.

I believe that Jesus highlights the lost most clearly in the Parable of the Sower, found in Matthew 13. The seed is sown, but it may have been on the path where it has quickly been eaten up by the birds (Mt. 13:4), it may have been sown among rocky ground and not have taken root (Mt.13:5), it may be among the thorns and have been choked out (Mt. 13:7).

Whatever the case, these people have heard the Gospel, but the world around them and their own decisions have robbed them of their faith. The seed of their faith in Christ has not taken root fruitfully. The Lost live hopeless lives, yet hope can be found right around the corner if they only had eyes to see it. Unlike the unreached, the lost generally have a Bible or have had one at some point in their lives, or at least they have access to one. It's just that the Word of God has not firmly taken root within them. Generally, we as believers and disciples of Jesus can spot the lost among a crowd of people. Their posture (physically and spiritually) may be hunched over. The spark placed in their eyes at birth has vanished; they are never content.

Our Necessary Role Among the Lost

I mentioned earlier that I spent roughly four years in the seminary discerning and receiving priestly formation. My time there was immensely blessed, yet filled with many heartaches and challenges. Perhaps one of the greatest heartaches was one Sunday morning when all of the seminarians took a large bus ride to a cathedral in Boston, MA. The year was 2004, and the scandals of priestly sexual misconduct and cover-ups were reaching an unsightly and horrible overflow in the Archdiocese of Boston. So many faithful Catholics of this diocese had been deeply wounded, whether they had actually been abused or not. People's faith in the Church, the priesthood, and even in Jesus Christ had been rocked.

As we pulled up to the cathedral, we encountered an enormous protest of people waiting outside the Church steps. Broken and enraged people were holding up signs and chanting things so as to get the attention of anyone who would listen. As we all exited the bus, I encountered a small and fragile woman standing off to the side; she was mute and deaf. She was holding up a sign that read, "I was sexually abused in the basement of this very Church!"

My heart broke, and as we were making our way into the Church, I just couldn't walk away from here. I had to turn back. I couldn't just walk by this woman like her pain and her brokenness didn't matter. I stopped and put my arm around her and pointed to my heart closing my eyes as if to say I was so deeply sorry for what happened to her. The screams and taunts of an active protest were swarming loudly around us; I just prayed she could experience and know Christ in and through our prayer. I humbly placed my arms on her shoulder and prayed for her. I was crushed. This woman was lost, and she was crying out for someone to help her. And sadly, it appeared as though perhaps her voice had been silenced and even dismissed for quite some time.

One thing that I often struggle to place inside my box of understanding God is that Jesus was a friend of sinners, lost and hurting people. They knew his name and often felt comfortable around Him. Apparently Jesus, who was free of any sin, was extremely comfortable around them as well. They came to Him with questions and sought his advice. That's an aspect of the character of Christ that humbles me so much. It seems that people who are outside of Church and not following Jesus daily don't often swarm toward me. I have much room to grow in this area. But not so for Jesus. We see the humility of Jesus welcoming sinners in scripture and God seems to even highlight it, from a lost woman involved in adultery (John 8:1-11) to Zacchaeus the crooked businessman who climbed a tall tree to see Him more clearly amid a crowd (Luke 19:1-10). Jesus was even deeply criticized by the scribes and Pharisees of his day for finding such comfort among sinners as they complained, "this man welcomes sinners and even eats with them" (Luke 15:2).

I feel the need to constantly ask myself the following questions: *Am I truly pursuing the lost? Are the lost comfortable in my presence like they were in the presence of Jesus? Do sinners know my name?* If my answer is "*not so much*" to these three questions, then I must ask myself, *why not*?

Years ago, I encountered the following thought by Philip Yancey while reading his work, *The Jesus I Never Knew*:

> *"The down and out, who flocked to Jesus when he lived on earth, no longer feel welcome. How did Jesus, the only perfect person in history, manage to*

attract the notoriously imperfect? And what keeps us from following in his steps today?"[34]

Perhaps one reason the lost are so lost and far from Christ is that many Christians are no longer pursuing people. I mean truly re-routing our days, dropping our plans, and pursuing people. Jesus pursued people and was generally interested in other people. He was deeply concerned when He encountered a man born blind; in fact, the entire ninth chapter of John's Gospel is devoted to it. He was sincerely interested in the life of Zacchaeus when He dined with him at his own home, and I have to be the same.

I must move away from the mentality that "people need to come to Jesus." We all know it is true that people need to come to Jesus, but what we fail to remember is that Jesus has commissioned all of us to go and bring them to Him. It's my task to bring them a clear and beautiful picture of who Jesus is.

I must now go where the lost are, and become interested in them and the things that capture their hearts. I must find them and see their dignity as Jesus saw the deep human dignity in the woman at the well. I must run after the lost and make it my mission to love them. Jesus loved and ransomed me "*while* I was still a sinner" (Romans 5: 8) and not one second after. I need to do the same to a world of lost people. Find them and love them. It's that simple. Then I can move forward from there. Once someone senses and understands that they are loved and dignified as a human being, they are generally eager to listen and learn.

Leaving Our Own Turf

When we lived in Central America, we spent almost an entire year inviting people to come to our Saturday night prayer service. The night included a free meal, drink, reading the Gospel, testimonies, prayer, and an encouraging invitation to join us for

Mass. There was a certain street in our town of people in need whom the Holy Spirit had placed on my heart. I walked their street, often inviting them to join us week after week, yet very few of them ever came.

I struggled with it. Eventually, I feel like the Holy Spirit gave me a vision of simply visiting them more and ultimately taking our weekly night to their street, bringing the Gospel to their doorstep. So that's what we did. We planned our night and packed everything up in our vans and headed out to their neighborhood with a bunch of our friends.

We filed into the dusty street and started singing songs about how great our God is. The Costa Rica heat had most people in their homes, away from the sun, but two by two, they started gathering out in the street to see what in the world was going on. Before much time, we had a great crowd of people lined up in the street to listen to the Gospel and to give God praise. I stood tall upon a ladder like Zacchaues did and reminded them how Jesus noticed Zacchaeus in a large crowd, and that Zacchaeus had great faith to step outside of his comfort zone to climb a tree to see Jesus.

It was a beautiful night to see them all gathered hearing the Gospel proclaimed, and because we went to them, it seemed like they were much more comfortable, and their ears and hearts seemed wide open. To my surprise, in the weeks to follow, many of them were finally coming to our Saturday night prayer services and some even to Mass.

What changed? The only change was we simply pursued them in their own homes. We *went* to them as Jesus had commanded us to do. We started speaking lovingly and freely to them and, more importantly, listening to them, and most importantly, we proved to them that the Gospel of Jesus was so important for us to share with them that we even took it to their neighborhood. We pursued them as Christ would pursue them, recklessly and without reservation.

Whether I want to admit it or not is up to me, but our Church is marred with sin and brokenness, but she is still the bride of Christ. Today many people carry a deep pain and lack of trust toward Christians of all faiths, especially Catholics. Sadly, we now live in an age where it is easy to dismiss an entire 2,000-year tradition of faith for the mistake of a single individual. We live in an age where it is far easier to criticize than to praise. It is my job as a baptized Catholic to proclaim love, truth, and mercy in these challenging times. Now is the time to be on the offensive end. Gone are the days when we could simply hang up Mass times and expect people to come and encounter the risen Lord. We are now living in the era of a Church in need of pursuing people because people are not necessarily pursuing the Church.

To Us Who Have Received So Much

"Go rather to the lost sheep of the house of Israel. When you go make this proclamation: the kingdom of God is at hand. Cure the sick, raise the dead, cleanse the lepers, drive out demons. Without cost you have received, without cost, you are to give."

– Matthew 10:6

If there is a scripture verse that has a tendency to haunt me or keep me uncomfortable, it is the one above. I, like many of you, am the recipient of so much. I attended Catholic schools, had a family that supported me and formed my conscience well as a Christian, and have had many mentors pour into and challenge me spiritually. Stop and think about all we have received from God. If, like me, you are a cradle Catholic, we have received grace upon grace our entire lives, real sanctifying grace. Think of all the Masses, talks, novenas, sacraments, retreats, homilies that we have all received. Even if you are a recent convert to Christ, what you have received is enormous. Our reception of all of this grace is not simply for our benefit alone. Christ calls us to go forth and find the lost sheep among us, not simply return home and repeat the same process next Sunday.

So often I am tempted to view my relationship with Christ and His Church as simply a recipient. Jesus commanding us to "go to the lost sheep" forbids me from remaining inside the Church where I am a comfortable recipient. I must go and joyfully give away that which I have received. This means that I must strategically find myself among the lost. I have to find ways to sincerely become friends to those far off from Christ because this is the heart of Jesus, to befriend the lost sinner. Do you want to witness great and immense rejoicing in heaven? Then go and befriend someone who is lost and apart from God and pour the love of Christ into them because "I tell you in just the same way there will be more joy in heaven over one sinner who repents than over ninety-nine righteous people who have no need of repentance" (Luke 15:7).

One of the greatest temptations for me is to spend much of my life surrounding myself with other Christians who are like minded with me. Don't get me wrong, having deep and meaningful fellowship and friendships with likeminded Christians is imperative, but it cannot define me. Having Christian community is the beginning and not the end. It is a temporary stop for me and not my permanent destination. My Christian community should be an experience of refueling only to be sent back out.

Consider the passage of the lost sheep in Luke 15:1-7, whereby Jesus leaves the ninety-nine to find the one missing sheep. If I constantly find myself among the comfort of ninety-nine righteous and never in pursuit of the one missing soul, then I am living contrary to the Gospel. I have to be willing to leave the comfort of my Christian community and pursue the lost. This is the Gospel example Jesus has set for me. Then, and only then, can I hear the great rejoicing in heaven over the return of the missing one soul.

Chapter 13: The Poor

"Let us touch the dying, the poor, the lonely and the unwanted according to the graces we have received and let us not be ashamed or slow to do the humble work." [35]

– St. Mother Teresa of Calcutta

It was a normal afternoon in Coopevega, Costa Rica, when I received a phone call from my friend Felipe. You remember him from an earlier chapter; he is the one who migrated from Nicaragua and lives in a dilapidated home with his handicapped wife Rosario. He was having trouble breathing, and I could immediately tell this from speaking with him.

"*Hermano, necisito ir al hospital! Algo esta malo.*" (Brother, I need to go to the hospital! Something is wrong.)

Escort into Paradise

For a few months, Felipe had been complaining about pain all over his body, namely his chest. He couldn't sleep well at night, and his breathing was troublesome. We took him to the hospital, as Lacy and I decided we needed to get a good x-ray to see what was going on. Health care out there is free for Costa Ricans, but for Nicaraguans with no papers like Felipe, it can be a great challenge and expense. Felipe sat shotgun with me up front, and he kept looking over his shoulder smiling at the kids in the back. I fixed a cup of coffee for myself before we left but saw him eyeing it, so I offered it to him. He accepted it with a huge smile. Van rides with our family can be like a circus or comedy act, and he was enjoying every minute of it, occasionally glancing back at the kids with his show-stopping smile. That image is seared permanently upon my heart.

I'll never forget the wide eyes and saddened look on the young doctor's face as he held up the x-ray to me over Felipe's shoulder. Felipe couldn't see it. The doctor shook his head in disbelief and gave me a cringe and sorrowful look. Felipe was essentially living on one lung; the other one was engulfed in fluid. The doctor told me that the situation was extremely urgent, and we needed to take him across the street to the public hospital for immediate care. I stated to him that I understood, and he looked at me and said, "No, sir, I want to make sure you truly understand; this is a dire emergency for your friend! Take him now!"

I walked Felipe across the street and as we were roughly twenty yards from the hospital entrance, he couldn't go anymore. He fell into my arms, gasping and fighting for air. I felt helpless. His body was like a wet noodle in my arms. I felt like everything was closing in on us. I screamed for someone to bring me a wheelchair, thinking my dear friend was about to die in my arms. I comforted him.

"*Estoy con ti, hermano; Jesus esta aqui tambien.*" (I am with you, brother; Jesus is here as well.)

By the grace of God, we received a wheelchair, and I escorted my gasping friend into the hospital. He could hardly breathe. They gave him oxygen and a bed in a room with twelve other people. The room smelled bad and had no privacy, as everyone was essentially watching each other in their pain. Finally, things had calmed down and Felipe would finally receive some care for this situation. I prayed with him a bunch, and we talked about great memories and smiled and laughed. His laugh is contagious, and the missing teeth in his smile display the adversity his life has pressed upon him.

I left the hospital to retrieve my family as we were going to head back home two hours away because the doctors told us he would be there for at least two weeks. Before leaving town, I felt the need to stop in one more time, so my daughter Norah and I ran inside and brought him some food. He was asleep but woke up when he sensed our presence. He simply smiled at us, a very peaceful and restful smile.

Norah and I laid our hands on him and prayed with him. We called the Holy Spirit upon him and asked Jesus to be with him at that moment. We told him we loved him, and he responded the same. As Norah and I walked away, I glanced over my shoulder into the crowded and loud public hospital to see my friend for what would be the final time.

Felipe died the next morning in the hospital. Our family was crushed. Telling his lovely wife, Rosario, that I was so sorry for her loss but that Felipe was now with Jesus seemed somewhat inappropriate, but as we swatted flies away from her stream of tears, we offered her hope and love. She laid in that bed with a thin, almost nonexistent mattress stained with dried urine and cried loud and enormous gut-wrenching tears. Her three-hundred-square-foot home was littered with trash and clothes and the flies were everywhere.

At this very moment, I realized that the poor have a lot in life that I will never come close to understanding. This reality was tremendously heightened as our sweet friend Rosario died just twelve days later in her sleep. She couldn't eat or sleep for a week after Felipe's passing, and eventually, she just passed away; perhaps she just couldn't handle living without her loving husband who cared for her with such a selfless and Christ-like love. We prepared and paid for funeral arrangements for her just twelve days after we did so for her husband Felipe. It was such a painful and somber time for their family, and our children shared in their sufferings as these beautiful people who they had come to love and serve had both passed away so quickly.

In much of Central America and all developing countries, there is no embalmment process, thus the body must be buried within twenty-four hours. Funerals and burials are not a sanitized and dressy formal occasion as they are in the developed world. Four men used a yellow rope I own and use in my evangelization talks to lower her body into a hole dug for her small coffin. It was a rainy day, and when they lowered the body, the moisture caused the coffin to slip off the rope and the entire coffin went tumbling down into the hole head first. Her deceased body tumbled out and the entire crowd of mourning friends and family looked away, gasping in terror. We pushed our children back to shield them from the traumatic scene.

I am sorry to share this story in such detail, but I do so to make the point that the poor suffer so many trials that you and I will never even be able to fathom. I feel like during this two-week journey, God reconfirmed deep within me that the poor are so worthy of our lives; they are worthy of our time, money, and especially our passion.

How to Serve the Poor

Many people come out here and visit us at our mission post serving alongside us for a week or so; this blesses us and the communities we serve tremendously. Generally, upon departing, they ask questions like, "How can I serve the poor back home like we did here this week?" While this can be a challenging question, it is one that we must ask ourselves, and ask it often. The poor are everywhere, and if I ignore them, I ignore Jesus Christ Himself. Remember Matthew 25, there will be a judgment, Jesus says so Himself, and we are the ones who will be judged, not the poor.

So many times in America I simply reduced the poor to those who refuse to work and be productive members of society. Sometimes that is true, sometimes it is not. I do not believe it is my priority to determine who is worthy to receive my help and who is not. Jesus never set that example for me. St. Ambrose so boldly states, "If you have two shirts in your closet, one belongs to you and the other to the man with no shirt."[36]

Sure, at some point, I must assess people's situation and see if I am truly helping them or not, but I must have the voice of Jesus resounding in my heart, "W*hatever you did for the least of my people, you did to me"* (Matthew 25:40). It really is that simple. Everyone, rich or poor, deserves the love of Jesus, and I as a Christian am called to bring it to them. There is no way around this Gospel reality.

Think of it this way. The deepest and most fundamental need of every single poor and marginalized person is Jesus. Can I not offer them Jesus and pray with them, listen to them, sit with them, and give them my eyes and ears? Can I not sit on the street with someone in need and sympathize with them during their pain? Everyone, rich or poor, deserves this. Once I have done this, I can be certain that I have fulfilled this person's greatest need because we are all spiritual beings.

Now I can move onto lesser, but still very important and often urgent, needs. Can I give you some food? Water? Coffee? Can I tend to your medical wounds? Would you like to talk to someone about your problem? Can I help you find shelter while you get back on your feet? These are extremely simple and basic needs that we all can assist with. We don't have to be multimillionaires to do this.

I just returned to my home from going to the store here in our small community. Two men who are alcoholics were sitting out front asking me for money, as they often do. Of course, I did not give them a handful of cash because I know they will go and spend it on alcohol. They have a horrible addiction. I know these men well, and I feed them at my home often. But I did buy them a soda and sit with them in front of the store for about twenty minutes.

I learned about how one has good work right now and the other does not. I learned that one's wife just left him and took their kids because he can't get himself together and stop drinking. I learned a few ways I can better serve them and their families this week. What did that cost me? Two dollars, twenty minutes, and an open heart. I have to serve the poor with everything I have, and I have been given a lot.

In the year 2017, Pope Francis instituted the first-ever World Day for the Poor whereby he celebrated Mass in St. Peter's Basilica and afterward hosted a lunch for roughly 1,500 poor people in the Paul VI Hall. The head chef in charge of Vatican meals served gnocchi, veal bites with vegetables, and tiramisu. These delicious items were served on fine white cloths and comfortable chairs. What an amazing expression of how we should treat the poor! On that day, the Church made a bold expression: the poor are deserving of our best, not just our leftovers. So what do I give the poor? My extra time when it's convenient? My leftover lunch? Can I give the poor my best? My Sunday family dinner with all its fine food and drink, topped off with gourmet coffee and dessert?

As we stood in the overgrown weeds and grass in the cemetery here in Coopevega, I was flooded with one hundred memories of Felipe and Rosario. My eyes welled up with tears as they often still do when I think of them. I remembered Rosario's belly laugh belting out as she held our newborn Andrew in her arms. She would cry when she laughed because her joy was at a climactic peak. I remembered sweating and eating popcorn with Felipe out of the same bowl on our front porch. We were the same, although our hands looked very different. He loved salted popcorn with coffee. I remembered the smiles on their faces and the joy in their hearts as we finished their new home. They finally had a concrete floor and a toilet. I remembered a trio of high school students from America who visited us and carried Rosario to the Church in their arms because she could not walk. She laughed so hard she cried on that evening as well. She was in the presence of Jesus, the real presence. Somehow, while owning nothing at all, her joy often brought her to tears.

These are the memories God had in store for my family and me when we first encountered Felipe and Rosario. The poor are not to be viewed as a hurdle in our day, but rather, as Pope Francis states, as "a passport to paradise."[37] I have to stop seeing the poor as a distraction and time-waster, and start seeing them as an opportunity to encounter Jesus. Which one of us deep down doesn't want to encounter Jesus? Felipe and Rosario were some of the poorest people I have ever encountered. Sometimes their needs could be seen as a distraction. They never had enough food. We built them a new floor, and then noticed the roof was leaking. But if our family would have just seen them as a distraction or a burden, we would have missed the beautiful relationship that God had in store for *us*. Perhaps the poor are the greatest blessing we can receive this side of heaven?

Sidestepping the Poor

Perhaps the biggest struggle I had while living in Central America was dealing with what is called diarios. A diario is essentially three to four days' worth of food, and the neediest people out there were always asking us for one. Imagine if you left a small bag of rice, beans, flour, oil, coffee, and perhaps some oats on your front porch. It would probably just sit there untouched for several weeks, maybe even the entire year. But out there, if I left a bag like that on my front porch, it would be gone in five minutes, and it might cause a fight between two families. A diario is what these people live on. I know, say goodbye to the American version of a carb-free healthy diet. The truth is while I am googling effective ways to eat healthier and improve my diet, the poor live on carbs because they are cheap and filling, and they usually don't have a refrigerator to store anything fresh.

People were constantly knocking on our door or running us down in the street asking us to give them a diario. At times, it was very rewarding, but quite honestly, many times it was overwhelming to field all the asks. However, the truth is many people there are hungry, and in a small farming town, when it is not harvesting time, there is often limited work, which means little to no food. I am embarrassed to tell you that I struggled with this because you would think it is so simple to just give a man or woman a bag of food. But it can be overwhelming, and I must admit that sometimes I try to sidestep the poor. You know what I mean, I'm sure? I try to avoid them because it is easier, more convenient, or because I have other plans that day.

Jesus is painfully clear to us about the poor. We just need to take a quick look at the story of the Rich Man and Lazarus found in Luke 16:19-31. You remember the story, the rich man dressed and dined finely while the poor man lay in his doorway. The scripture states that Lazarus would have gladly eaten the scraps that fell from the rich man's table. The only other piece of information that Jesus is concerned with giving us is that dogs used to lick Lazarus' wounds then He goes on to make his main point. When they die, the rich man goes down to the netherworld to suffer torment in flames while Lazarus was carried away by angels into heaven. I believe it is important for us to hone in on what Jesus says about these two men and try to get to the bottom of what Jesus is telling us in the parable.

First off, in introducing the rich man, Jesus gives us no other information other than the fact that he dressed in fine garments and dined sumptuously. I would find great comfort and even some personal separation from this rich man had Jesus mentioned that he was a royal jerk, a money launderer, and spent his money on fast drugs and loose women. But nowhere does Jesus state these things. The rich man is sent to eternal torment and all Jesus wants us to know about him is that he was rich, dressed and dined finely, and stepped around an extremely poor man at his door each day. Jesus seems to be exposing the vice of living in luxury, and doing so much so that we avoid and even forget the poor. I can relate to that. I am often guilty of that.

In his sermon "On Wealth and Poverty," St. John Chrysostom states, "For as the rich man lived in such wickedness, practiced luxury every day, and dressed himself splendidly, he was preparing for himself a more grievous punishment, building himself a greater fire, and making his penalty inexorable and his retribution inaccessible to pardon."[38] We are all guilty in some regard of the pursuit of luxury, and it is an empty pursuit. Its promises are enormous and its fruits are bitter and lifeless. But how can I see the poor when I am pursuing my own success, pursuing my next luxurious destination in life? I, like the rich man, so easily step over the poor Lazarus daily.

Am I Really Rich?

But we don't view ourselves as rich, do we? In my mind, there are always tons of people richer than I am, plenty of people pursuing greater luxuries than I am. But this is not how God sees us. We are the richest people to ever inhabit the planet in arguably one of the richest periods of the history of this planet. We are wealthy. If you and I are holding this edited and printed book in a house or building with the amenities of electricity, running water, sewer, and air conditioning, I am here to tell you that we are one of the world's wealthiest people.

It's okay because becoming self-aware is one of the biggest steps to our understanding of how we can serve the poor. When our family moved to Central America, one of my closest friends offered to send me a window air conditioning unit. In America, we often scoff at a window unit because it isn't a central AC unit. I had to decline it because not one person in our Central American town had an AC unit of any type in their home. It's almost unheard of.

So yes, you and I are rich. You and I are filthy, rolling around in our richness rich. But that can be an enormous blessing to you and me as well because if we have plenty of riches, then we can give plenty to the poor. It is indeed that simple. On the other hand, if we simply consume our riches for ourselves and step around the poor, then Jesus details our final destination in Luke 16.

Let's Serve the Poor with Gladness!

Now is the time to give most or all we have to the poor, earn treasure in heaven, and follow Jesus. These thoughts are not my original thoughts, they are those of Jesus, and too often we dismiss them. Sure He looks at a rich young man in the eye in Mark 10 and tells him to do this, but I believe he is calling many of us to do the same today.

Just imagine it. If we weren't so bound up by our pursuits of riches and conveniences, we would have more time, passion, and richness for the poor. St Ambrose states, "There is your brother, naked, crying, and you stand their confused over the choice of an attractive floor covering."[39] I don't recall this quote to guilt any of us into serving the poor, I just quote it to remind myself that my daily interests and passions are not often that of Christ. Buying a new house, changing wall colors, or upgrading my boat are not all that important at all to God. Jesus was and is wildly in love with the poor and with serving them with joy and gladness. When I encounter the poor, I too, like St. Ambrose, can finally have the eyes to see how stupid and meaningless my daily pursuits can be. Mother Teresa reminds us that serving the poor is the noblest of tasks. This quote, often attributed to her, captures this so well, "At the end of life, we will not be judged by how many diplomas we have received, how much money we have made, how many great things we have done. We will be judged by 'I was hungry, and you gave me something to eat; I was naked, and you clothed me. I was homeless, and you took me in.'" The truth is we are called to serve the poor because Jesus has called us to. We can bargain and excuse ourselves out of it, but at the end of the day, Jesus demands this of us. Sure, it can be taxing, but truth be told, there is enormous joy in serving the poor.

Restoring Justice

As I explained earlier, while living in Costa Rica, just about every single Saturday at 5:30 p.m., you could find our family serving a free meal and praying with the poor of Coopevega. God placed upon our hearts to "feed people" when we arrived here, and the Holy Spirit turned that vision into a free weekly meal, a few praise songs, and a brief talk or testimony after the weekly Gospel proclaimed to anyone who wants to come. No cost and no requirements; just come and be fed.

It became an amazing thing for us to witness as God brought people from various stages and walks of life together on those Saturday nights. Most of them don't have much, and they are so grateful. Our goal is to simply love them for who they are, feed them spiritually, and of course feed their bellies. For some of them, it is the most meat they will eat all week. We always invited them to the 7:00 p.m. Mass at our Church next door, and eventually, several of them came. Most of these people are non-Catholic, but I believe they sense something greater than themselves is occurring next door on the altar.

While living in Costa Rica, we usually fed anywhere from forty to eighty people each Saturday evening before Mass. It was great and even rewarding at times. But in the grand scheme of things, we didn't pat ourselves on the back at the end of these nights, because we simply felt like the servants in Luke 17:10: "When you have done all you have been commanded, say, 'We are unprofitable servants; we have done what we were obliged to do.'"

The Church of Jesus Christ calls each one of us to restore justice to the poor. Have you ever pondered exactly what that means for us? To restore justice means to restore or return to someone that which belongs to them. St. Ambrose is famously noted for the following quote that throws a dart at my pride each time I hear it: "It is not from your own possessions that you are bestowing alms on the poor, you are restoring to them what is theirs by right."[40]

In my opinion, this quote sums up justice. If I have three sandwiches and you have none, and I give you one, then I am merely restoring justice to you. Why would I need to have three sandwiches? Why would I want to have three sandwiches when I am looking at you sitting next to me longing for just one sandwich? In essence, this is what we were striving to do every Saturday night, to simply restore a bit of justice to the poor.

These people are physically and spiritually hungry and not many people are standing in line to offer them what they need. Far too often, I can make the unnecessary jump and think, *well then that man should get out and make some money and buy himself a sandwich.* While there may be some truth to this statement, in a world of 7 billion people, not everyone will have the opportunity that you and I have to get out there and make some money. So the

Church calls us to restore justice to the poor and to spend the rest of our lives doing so.

I have found that when I strive to restore justice, it doesn't cost me much. Remember the example: three sandwiches, what in the world am I going to do with three sandwiches at lunch? Justice is giving out of my excess, and looking around and within myself, I see tremendous excess at my disposal. Do I really need a flat screen television in every room of our home? Although I enjoy it, and there is nothing wrong with it, do I need to eat out every single Saturday evening?

The scary reality for me is that when we moved out into the jungles of rural Costa Rica, so many of the things in my life that I was accustomed to turned out to be things that most of these people had never experienced before. Simple amenities like air conditioning an entire house for twenty-four hours a day, a dryer, and a microwave. Is it bad to own these things? Not at all, but I am coming to understand that they are not necessary; they are excess and luxury items for the majority of people on this planet.

So perhaps God will call me to give away my third sandwich, and that won't even really register to me as restoring justice. But what about when God asks me to do away with my cable package, a summer house, or my frivolous spending? What if He is asking me to do away with these things because the sun will set today in Asia and a vast number of people will not have eaten? Wouldn't it make me sleep better knowing that a few more children had breakfast because I made a decision to give away some of what I have?

Moving Deeper: From Justice to Love

Restoring justice is giving from our excess; none of us here in the Western world will starve if we simply choose to restore justice by giving from our excess. If I don't do it, then who will?

The next way in which God will call us to give is a radical calling, but indeed not an uncommon way for God to call us at all. Sometimes God, who is love Himself, will move us beyond restoring justice and into loving someone. When we love someone, we give not only from our excess but we choose to give from our need. There is an enormous difference. Perhaps this simple story told by St. Teresa of Calcutta states it best:

> *"Some time ago a man came to our house and he said, 'Mother, there is a family, a Muslim family, that has eight children. They have not eaten for a long time. Do something for them.' So, I took some rice and I went. When I arrived at their house I could see the hunger in the children's eyes. Their eyes were shining with hunger. I gave the rice to the mother, and she took the rice. She divided it into two, and then she went out. When she came back, I asked her, 'Where did you go?' She said, 'They are hungry also. Next door neighbor, they were also hungry.' What struck me most, not that she gave the rice but she knew they were hungry. And because she knew, she shared. And this is what we have to come to know . . . Love, to be true, has to hurt and this woman who was hungry—she knew also that her neighbor was also hungry."* [41]

To love is to give out of my need, and that hurts and costs me something. Restoring love is even greater than restoring justice. Both are great and both are required of us, but in this manner, how many times can I say that my gift was a true act of love? I may write a check and support a certain ministry, but my day can go on basically like I never wrote that check.

Another example I like to use is that one time our family identified a family in need of a home as they were living with two other families at the time in a one-bedroom home. We checked our mission fund (we are 100 percent dependent upon donations to live and serve as foreign missionaries), and we had the amount needed to build a home. We built the $3,000 all-wood home, and not one person who contributed to our family's mission fund felt it.

Do you understand my point? We built a family of six a home in a poor community and no one had to make any enormous sacrifice. Because everyone who donated to us essentially donated from their excess. It was an amazing outpouring of love upon this family, and it was so easy for all of our mission team to do. We didn't even feel its financial effects upon us.

Many times, I simply give from my excess, and many times, I see and feel God calling me to give out of love, self-donation, and I tense up. I tense up because it requires so much more of me. Jesus gave out of love, and it cost Him everything. He set the glorious example for us to follow, yet so often we tense up and run in the other direction. Sometimes love requires us to give not only one of our three sandwiches away, but sometimes love requires us to give all three away, and that is so much deeper than justice.

We are called to love as well, each one of us in a different but also similar type of way. We are called to give until it hurts, and then allow Christ to show us how to give even more. We have come a long way in this chapter from the rich man and Lazarus, but looking back on that rich man, how horrible of an existence did he have? His days were filled with feeding and caring for himself alone. More and more each day, I sense God calling me not to get caught up in my plans and possessions. There is a pressure and tug I can feel within me.

I encourage you to recall the moment you first had an encounter with the living God, the first time your heart was truly set on fire. Do you remember how you felt God's pursuit of you? He pursued you with a reckless abandon, a sinner and all. He left heaven to chase after you, a sinner. I encourage you, as I encourage myself, to pursue the poor in our world with such reckless abandonment. What can I leave behind, what excess in my life can I live without, if it means I can serve the poor more directly? What changes in my life can I make to be more available to Jesus in the poor?

Let's spend time among the poor, real time, precious time. Time that we could be spending on other things. Strive to spend the same amount of time with Jesus in the poor as we try to spend with Jesus in the Eucharist. Is it not the same Christ after all? The poor have a way of existing outside of time, it seems. Have a real meal with them, don't just serve a meal to them, but serve yourself out of the same serving bowl as them. Sit down with them. Eye to eye.

I can remember how Felipe used to come and sit on our porch and ask Lacy to make popcorn. I had this natural tendency to just give everyone their own paper plate or napkin of popcorn. But for some reason, on this day, there were no paper plates, and Lacy brought out only two bowls of popcorn: one for the kids and one for her, Felipe, and me. We finally ate popcorn out of the same bowl. It was awesome. Felipe is now gone, and all I have is his legacy within me and an old, blue mesh cap of his that his family gave to me as a gift. Truthfully, I would give just about anything to eat popcorn out of the same bowl with Felipe just one more time. One more visit with Jesus on my front porch.

Chapter 14: The Unreached

"Many, many people hereabouts are not becoming Christians for one reason only: there is nobody to make them Christians."[42]

– St Francis Xavier

The day was hot and thick with humidity and I was in great awe. A once far-off concept was now becoming a reality. I found myself being escorted by two priests in an SUV through very dusty, deep back roads of the Muslim country of Bangladesh. There were people everywhere, hundreds, thousands, millions. I was finally becoming able to grasp the truth that in a world of over 7 billion people, nearly one-third of them do not know Jesus.

Less than 1 percent of the population of Bangladesh professes Jesus Christ as king.[43] To be honest, I just couldn't grasp that statistic before arriving. It seemed impossible for someone like me who grew up in a Christian nation. But here I was being shown so many people who most likely had no earthly clue who Jesus Christ was.

They were working tirelessly in the fields that surrounded us; earning only $0.90 per day. The world as I knew it was changing in my mind. Who will present the Gospel to these beautiful people? Who will proclaim the hope and love of Jesus Christ to a people so far from Him? What happens if these people live and die without ever having the Gospel proclaimed to them?

To the Nations . . . ALL of Them

It's challenging to sum up in words everything that I experienced in Bangladesh, but perhaps the following statement from our beautiful Church can shed great light on it:

> *"The Church, which has been sent by Christ to reveal and communicate the love of God to all men and to all peoples is aware that for her, a tremendous missionary work remains to be done. There are two billion people—and their number is increasing day by day—who have never, or barely heard, the Gospel message; they constitute large and distinct groups united by enduring cultural ties, ancient religious traditions, and strong social relationships. If the Church is to be in a position to offer all men the mystery of salvation and the life brought by God, then it must implant itself among all these groups in the same way that Christ and his incarnation committed himself to the particular social and cultural circumstances of the men among whom he lived."*[44]

I was realizing that up to this point in my life I had not really seen the urgent need to go and evangelize in these Christian minority countries, and I had certainly not glanced at the intense spiritual need in these countries. In our digital and informed age, it is hard to imagine, but there exists in our world what we refer to as unreached people groups; people who are indeed unreached in terms of receiving the Gospel. These groups are what Jesus is referring to in the scriptures when He commands us to "go to all nations" (Matthew 28:19). These groups are different from nations or countries as we know it. In fact, there are only 195 countries in the world, yet there are roughly 17,097 people groups in the world, making up a population of over 7 billion people and counting.[45]

For instance, the country of India alone has over 1 billion people and contains 2,605 people groups, of which 2,330 have still not received the Gospel fruitfully.[46] Of the world's 17,097 people groups, roughly 42 percent, or 7,148, are unreached people groups.[47] These are people who do not have a substantial Christian presence among them that can fruitfully transmit the faith within its own population. The Catholic Church has long referred to mission work among these people groups as "Mission Ad Gentes"[48] as this term means "to the nations."

The Church further identifies a great need for our reaching these peoples by stating that mission Ad Gentes is "essential and never-ending,"[49] and even more so by declaring "now is the time to devote all of the Church's energies to a new evangelization and to the mission ad gentes."[50] Thus, the Great Commission of Christ to preach the Gospel to *all* nations is far from complete and still holds the place of primacy in the life of the Church.

The 10/40 Window / A Window of Despair

But we can't find these people in our own backyards; to reach them with the Gospel, we have to leave and go. And we have to go far. The majority of the unreached people groups reside in what is referred to as the 10/40 window, a term coined by Christian Mission Strategist Luis Bush. Basically, if you would take a world map and draw a line in the eastern hemisphere also including Europe and Africa in the west and mark off the territory from 10-40 degrees north of the equator, you would highlight the 10/40 window.[51] This is the window of the world that desperately cries out for the heart, time, talent, energy, and resources of our Church today; yet, this is the window that receives the least amount of the above. Roughly two-thirds of the entire world's population lives in this section of the world. Not only is this highlighted area defined by a lack of access, reception, and knowledge of the Gospel of Jesus Christ, this area is also defined by the greatest needs in terms of poverty and overall socioeconomic challenges.

On top of these challenges, these people are unreached because of the many challenges and dangers of reaching them. Corrupt and extreme government, heavy persecution, and the threat of radical terrorism loom around the corner in many of these nations. They are unreached for a reason. While the Church is present, and even vibrant and thriving in a few small areas within this window, as a whole, the Gospel has yet to fully take root there; it is a window of despair.

After only my first day in Bangladesh I realized that even though the bishops, priest, religious, and laity were so faithful there, the sad reality is that there is still a tremendous amount of work to be done in these nations. I was realizing that what Pope John Paul II stated, "the mission is still only beginning,"[52] was so painfully accurate. I felt a deep stirring and a deep desire to love and serve these people. I had come to Bangladesh in hopes of discovering exactly what kind of need there was in the 10/40 Window and to see if our family could serve fruitfully in Asia, and my questions were answered instantly with a resounding *yes*. Now was the time.

But There is So Much Need Here . . . In Our Own Backyard.

So often I hear, "But why would you go and serve somewhere else when there is so much need here in America." I have come to simply cringe when I hear this statement, and I realize that no single phrase better sums up our lack of understanding of the Great Commission of Jesus Christ. And truly that's all it really is: a lack of a global understanding. In America, we have resource upon resource to evangelize, catechize, serve the poor, and equip our Church for generations to come. In many parts of India, with its population of over 1 billion people, there is often no sign of a Church, let alone resources for catechesis and service.

One extremely hot and muggy Saturday afternoon while visiting Bangladesh, I left my hotel room to go to Mass. Despite having directions and a smartphone, I could not find the Church, which was only a mere half a mile walk from my hotel. I kept walking and kept searching in this enormous city. I kept asking the people around me where this Church was. I was absolutely perplexed; not only could I not find the Church, but no one around me living in this neighborhood had even heard of the Church. After forty-five minutes of walking and questions, the rain started coming down in sheets; it was monsoon season. I was drenched and quite frustrated. I felt like an idiot and went back to my hotel room and Ubered a ride there.

The same thing happened with my Uber driver. He drove and drove, passing the same locations I had recently walked, and had no clue where to find the Church. He asked around, and everyone shook their head in confusion. I was no longer in America where there was a well-known Church on nearly every corner. Eventually, we found the Church, it was hidden behind an enormous concrete wall, with barb wire and armed guards protecting the gate. It became clear to me that in this megalopolis of Dhaka, Bangladesh, most of its 15 plus million inhabitants did not know Jesus. I thought to myself, *it is for this reason that I would go and serve somewhere else when there is so much need here in America.*

We believe we have so much need in America, and perhaps we do, but what we often forget is how many resources we have in America. Resources both physical and spiritual. But our Church is so enormous and universal. There are thousands of small village chapels scattered across the world with such great material and spiritual need. Most parishes in America probably have a post-Mass coffee and donut budget that is greater than many of these small village chapels in Asia and Africa would receive to operate completely all year long. I am not saying these things to indict our American Church; I'm simply making the statement in hopes that perhaps our perspective may change regarding the universality of the Church.

We have so many resources in Christian America. Beautiful new churches being built, top of the line sound systems to amplify our Gospel to the masses of people, and beautiful, comfortable, adorned churches for people who hear the Gospel proclaimed every single week to sit in. We can renovate our churches when we feel they are old, or build great and beautiful new ones after asking for donations to do so. We have been blessed by God with so much.

For two years, we served in rural Central America. Many of the surrounding pueblos or towns have no catechist, no marriage prep, no confirmation or RCIA courses; some don't even have a married Catholic couple in their town to be a godparent, thus my wife and I are godparents to several of these children. The churches are generally made of second-hand wood and nails, and I have yet to see a sound system. For this reason, I would "go and serve somewhere else when there is so much need here in America." The fundamental, yet often hard to admit truth, for most of us American Christians is that, while there may be a great and important spiritual and physical need here in America for us to engage in, these needs pale greatly in comparison to the needs of the rest of the world. It's true and it's tough for me to stomach.

We have so many pursuits and outreaches happening in our American Churches, and many of them are so necessary and fruitful, but by and large, we have forgotten about preaching the Gospel *ad gentes*. We cater to young adults and youth, young married couples and singles, veterans, and immigrants, but we turn our hearts and attention away from the unreached; those who have never heard the Gospel. We are living our lives as though everyone on earth has heard the Gospel, and everyone on earth is receiving the sacraments, but this is so far from the truth. In fact, according to Wycliffe Bible Translators, there are roughly 1,600 languages who don't even have a Bible translation in their native tongue.[53] Stop and think about that for a moment.

The Great Commission of Jesus Christ is far from complete. But our approach doesn't have to be an either/or one. We can still serve our donuts and coffee after Mass. We can still serve the great and pressing needs of the youth and young adults of our American parishes while reaching out to the nations; in fact, we should be equipping the youth and young adults in our parish to reach the unreached in foreign nations. But as a whole, we are not. Yet.

Sinking Ships Among Us

Perhaps I can paint a picture of an analogy that may better illumine my point. Imagine for just a moment that you are out at sea as part of an ocean rescue team somewhere in the middle of the Pacific Ocean. Your crew has been abruptly called up in the middle of the night to rescue a sinking ship with hundreds of people on board. As you arrive, your heart sinks as you discover the majority of people floating in the ocean being tossed about by the enormous waves. Lives are being lost at a rapid pace, and those who are being saved are in peril condition. You and your crew completely forget about yourselves as you are plunged into the selfless efforts of rescuing those who are perishing. You land several survivors onto your rescue ship whereby they can receive vital treatment, warm clothes, and immediate, necessary medical treatment. After a long, tiresome night, you and your crew finally can take a deep breath as most of the dire needed rescue work has been done.

Yet suddenly over the radio, the captain of the ship gets information that this particular ship is not the only ship lost and wrecked at sea. In fact, there is another ship. No, another five ships. No, there are hundreds more sinking ships filled with people who are now lost at sea perishing.

This first boat has been stabilized, and the people have been rescued and brought back to life. The people are in good shape because they have received the primary attention. They have been the beneficiaries of so many resources and in such a timely manner. But what about the other ships? These ships are still out there sinking. The people once aboard these ships are now drowning in the Pacific Ocean, and they have no hope of being saved.

Wouldn't it make perfect sense for you and your crew to take most of your rescue men and women and move onward to those who are still in the roaring sea lost and drowning? Or do you think the more prudent thing to do would be for all of us to continue to spend all of our time and resources helping those in the first sinking ship? Sure, some of us could and should stay behind and help those on the first ship, but many of us should go out and seek those that are still so lost and without hope.

And such is the case with the Church in today's world. There are literally billions of human beings who are lost at sea and perishing because they have not yet heard the Gospel of Jesus Christ, and there aren't many willing to abandon their current plans and face the stormy sea directly to rescue them. But it doesn't have to be this way.

Finishing the Great Commission / Should We *All* Go?

Thank God there is still daylight and that we are still alive because the Great Commission is far from finished; we still have so much work to do. Jesus says Himself in the Gospel of Mark 13:10,

"The Gospel must be preached first to all nations," before he returns. And praise God that you and I have the opportunity to be a part of that. I don't know about you, but when He returns, I want to be found doing His will and spreading His Gospel, searching for those who need Him most. But as a Church, we have to be extremely intentional in our planning to reach the unreached if we are to obey the final words of Christ in making disciples of all nations.

So does this mean that every single one of us must stop what we are doing, put all else in our lives on hold, and Go? Well, perhaps so, for some of us. It does indeed mean that for us to take Jesus and His greatest command of us as believers seriously, we must stop and discern whether or not He is inviting us into this type of service. So a resounding *yes* to the question *should more of us go?* For Lacy and me, there has been nothing more fulfilling and glorious than following Jesus onto the unknown waters of the unreached people groups of the world.

You may be reading this chapter and asking yourself, "Well, I live in America and probably always will; what in the world can I do to make a difference in reaching the unreached?"

Be a Sender/Supporter

Saint Mother Teresa is often credited with saying, "Some go by giving and some give by going." What a great and beautiful quote that beckons all of us into the heart of the Great Commission. Essentially, she is saying that each one of us by virtue of our baptism is required to be involved in the completion of the Great Commission. If you find yourself reading this book or hearing the words of Jesus Christ to all of us telling us to Go to the nations, yet after discernment, you are convinced to stay, then it is your mission to be a sender to the unreached.

A sender is someone who is quite possibly just as involved in actually going as the one who leaves to serve. There are an unfathomable amount of details and hurdles to fruitfully place a missionary onto the mission field within the 10/40 Window today. Issues such as visas, education, financial support, emotional and psychological support, prayer dependency, legal work, and on and on it goes. For every missionary that serves in the mission field, there must be close to one hundred people behind him/her on a team of multifaceted support.

Each week at our home base in America, our mission organization, Family Missions Company, commits to spending the morning praying for those who send and support missionaries around the world. The list is enormous from donors to family members, and they truly are the backbone of sending and keeping missionaries in the mission field. These are the people who are diligently packing and sustaining a missionary's bag, making sure they have everything they need physically, spiritually, and emotionally. These people play an enormous and necessary role.

I'll never forget the first time we returned from the mission field. We had been serving in Central America for a year and came home during Christmas time. Some of our closest personal friends approached us and said, "We are throwing you all a party with all your friends whether you like it or not. Just send us a list of people you want there." This type of love and hospitality works miracles to the missionary who has been away from family and home. It was one of the many ways they supported us and packed our bag while we served as foreign missionaries.

When we arrived, we were greeted by our dearest of friends who were there to reaffirm that they were indeed supporting us. We laughed with one another, prayed together, and shared the many ways we had seen the face of God in the foreign field of missions.

So ask yourself a question: who am I supporting or sending to reach those who have never heard the Gospel? If the answer is no one, then start there. Find someone and lovingly and prayerfully support them.

Prayer and Fasting

Just this year during lent, I pleaded with God to reveal to me ways in which I and my family could fruitfully share the Gospel with those whom we live with here in Asia. Being in a Muslim country has so many challenges. It is illegal to share the Gospel with Muslims, and it is illegal for them to receive the Gospel and convert to Christ. The challenges and issues sometimes appear to be deeper than the sea. But God's love and desire for these people is even far deeper.

I sensed the Holy Spirit calling me to a fast during Ramadan, the month that Muslims pray and fast so intensely. Further, I felt a calling to reach out to several of our committed prayer warriors and financial donors asking them to be a part of this fast. After only one request, I had about twenty people signed up to fast and pray with me during Ramadan. It was amazing. We were all scattered across the world, yet bonded through fasting and prayer for the Holy Spirit to touch all Muslim people across the world so that they could receive the Gospel of Jesus Christ fruitfully and that doors would be opened for us to fruitfully serve these beautiful people as a family.

In just the first week, our family witnessed breakthroughs. People who we hadn't shared the Gospel with heard the good news from us. We became friends with a Muslim family within our neighborhood, and I was asked to pray with a Hindu man with a heart problem in a crowded restaurant filled with Muslim people. I believe when we seek God and his faithfulness through fasting and prayer, we will see it and receive it. But all of that grace came as a result of a decided fast by many people who were still working their nine-to-five jobs as missionary disciples in America. They were teachers, physicians, insurance salesmen, and local pastors. But together, we are all missionaries serving in the 10/40 window. Our prayer and fasting during Ramadan mattered to God, and He heard the cry of our heart: that many Muslim people who don't regularly hear the Gospel would hear it.

My encouragement and challenge is to take one day each week and beg God in prayer and fasting that people who have never heard the Gospel of Jesus Christ will somehow have the means to do so. Ask for the Holy Spirit to rain down showers of grace upon these unreached people groups. Ask for Bible translations among the thousands of people whose languages are still in darkness since the tragedy at Babel. Beg the Holy Spirit to send them the Word of God. As your stomach growls and you want to eat, cry out loud to Jesus, "My Lord, I love you and your beloved people across the world more than this meal. Please honor this fast and may your Gospel break through into the hearts of people around the world who do not know you yet!"

I beg you to consider: Is this an urgent matter? The fact that 3 billion people don't know Jesus, does that not stir something within your heart as a baptized Christian disciple of Jesus Christ? The world needs Jesus, and you and I have the power and resources to share Christ with the unreached if only we would lean deeply into the Holy Spirit and ask Him to move.

Most Importantly, Go!

"If God calls you to be a missionary, don't stoop to be a king."

– Jordan Groomes

If you think God is calling you to foreign missions, especially among unreached peoples of the world, stop thinking and Go! The unreached are the most forgotten people in the world. As Christians, we dedicate so much time, talent, energy, and resources to so many different and worthy causes, but by and large, we dedicate almost nothing to the unreached.

Consider the disparity of these global facts: Only .02 percent of all Christian Missionaries are serving among the unreached. There is a ratio of 1 Christian missionary for every 450,555 Muslims.[54] Many people may respond by saying something like, "Well, perhaps God isn't calling people to serve in those areas . . ." Would it be the case that God would call 99 percent of us to stay in America and serve those who have already heard the Gospel, and only call 1 percent of us to go and live and serve among the unreached?

This is not to minimalize the necessity for local evangelism in America and among the reached nations. It is imperative to evangelize there and to re-evangelize. But the heart of Christ bleeds for His people, and close to three billion of them has yet to hear about Him. What will we do as a Church, what will you and I do as individuals? If Christ is calling you to bring the Gospel to those who have never heard it, then by all means, don't ever even consider stooping low to be a king.

The mission organization the Traveling Team states that of all the money received by Christians across all denominations in America only 1 percent is used on the unreached.[55] That means that as a whole, as a Church, we are spending 99 percent of our resources either on ourselves in America or sending it to those nations who have already heard the Gospel. While there is no need to fault the Church for spending resources in America and other reached nations, now is certainly the time to ask why we are only spending 1 percent on the unreached.

There Are So Many More Sinking Ships

I don't think anything could have prepared me for what I experienced in Bangladesh. I had flown out there alone to meet with a few bishops in hopes of moving our family there to set up a full-time mission post, but because of many hurdles, we simply could not move there as a family at that time. Perhaps the Holy Spirit will open up a door in the future for us to walk through. I spent much of my time there traveling around in a rickshaw—which is a small metal-type cage on the rear of a bicycle.

From my humble view, I could take in the thick smog, horns, and constant noise . . . Horns cried out so loudly as cars were stuck bumper to bumper as far as my eyes could see. There were people everywhere in this city, in cars, walking, on bikes. A human traffic jam best describes Dhaka. Being from Louisiana, I could say it reminded me of Mardi Gras, but on a much larger and permanent scale. I had never seen a city so dense in population, and I had never seen anything like this place.

Bangladesh is home to roughly 170,000,000 people, and about 15,000,000 of those people all live in Dhaka. It is a mega-city. Of the roughly 170,000,000 people living in Bangladesh, about 50,000,000 of them are living below the poverty line. For many people in Bangladesh, poverty means living in slums made of metal and cardboard, drinking water that is far below sanitized standards, and struggling to eat each day. I experienced these realities as I traveled to each corner of the country meeting people and trying my best to soak in all the country had to offer.

The crazy thing is that Bangladesh is simply one small corner of the world of unreached people groups. There are so many small and large pockets of people still longing and waiting for the Gospel and the love and mercy of Jesus Christ. There are so many places like Bangladesh within the 10/40 window. Most of them are hard to get to and even harder to remain in. But now is the time. Now is the time for us to ask the Lord of the harvest to send more workers into the vineyard, for there are so many sinking ships around us.

Chapter 15: Let's Go. Now Is the time!

"Let us go forward in peace, our eyes upon heaven, the only one goal of our labors."[56]

– St. Therese of Lisieux

If you are still reading, then you are closer to your death then you were the day you picked up this book. Such a morbid thought, I know. But we are all passing away, and there is nothing we can do to stop the process. Our days are numbered, and what will the rest of them look like? Are we willing to give our lives away to Jesus in a new and radical way and walk humbly and consistently with Him daily? Can we be humble and courageous, and dive deeper into the ocean of love that is Jesus Christ? Our time on earth is so short, and our relationships with others are not guaranteed to last much longer.

I'll never forget watching poor Costa Rican men lower my dear friend Felipe down into the wet and muddy earth with my yellow rope. Tears streamed down my face as I thought, *Man, I still had so much to share with him, and he still had so much to share with the world!* But we are reminded of this reality throughout scripture, "Teach us to count our days aright, that we may gain wisdom of heart" (Palm 90:12), "For all flesh is like grass, and all its glory like the flower of the field; the grass withers, and the flower wilts; but the word of the Lord remains forever" (1 Peter 1:24), and finally, "We have no idea what our lives will be like tomorrow. You are a puff of smoke that appears briefly and then disappears" (James 4:14).

Be a Doer of the Word

So often in my life I read something, listen to a talk or homily, or experience God in some new and profound way and feel a deeper conviction in my faith. *I'm going to do this, and I'm going to do that!* I declare to myself. Sadly, sometimes it remains simply that, a conviction, and I don't act on it. I have found in my life that there is always a small window of opportunity for me to act upon a conviction. This is when my mind is most alert and my spirit is renewed; it is the time for action and not only talk and conviction.

Imagine if we sat in Church one Sunday morning and heard a heart-filled presentation to help sex-trafficked children in Asia. I am 100 percent certain that everyone would leave the Church convicted to do something about it. "Imagine if those children were our children," we would say to our spouse as we drove off back to our homes to eat lunch. But our convictions mean absolutely nothing if we return back home and conduct life as usual.

Our convictions to help these vulnerable children will remain with us for about twenty-four hours or so, and then they will fade away to nothing like so many of our other past convictions. We generally just move on to other normal daily pursuits; that's just how we are conditioned as humans. Perhaps we would bring it up on Monday at work when someone asks us how our weekend went. Convictions are empty and meaningless until we act upon them.

The letter of James states it best, "Be doers of the word and not hearers only, deluding yourselves. For if anyone is a hearer of the word and not a doer, he is like a man who looks at his own face in the mirror. He sees himself, then goes off and promptly forgets what he looked like" (James 1:22-24).

Sadly, too often in my life I have felt convictions, talked about them to my friends and family, and then just let them fade away without my taking action. I have often been a hearer of the word and not a doer of the word.

Imagine our lives ending and God showing us this enormous pile of smoking ashes.

"What's that pile of ashes, Lord?"

"Oh, that's the pile of your burnt out and dead convictions. Look, right there is when you were convicted to get into shape, that small pile is when you were convicted to read the entire Bible, this one here is when you were convicted to adopt a child, and that one over there is when you were going to start giving more of your time to me. But you actually did none of those things."

Instead of that horrendous scene, I prefer to walk with God in heaven and Him show me all the bright-hot burning fires that have now become a full blaze because of my convictions. Can you imagine that scene?

"Look, my son, these are all the children you fed with your simple monthly donation at Church all those years; this is the home you built for the family in Africa; they lived their entire life in it and now their grandchildren are in it. Look over here; because you started to read the Bible every day, all of your children are doing so now, and their hearts are now set on fire for me. You were a doer of the word while you were on earth, and here is some of the fruit. Taste its richness."

Go Now

Almost every week, my wife and I try our best to communicate to our children that this life is passing, but eternity is forever. It's such a hard concept to grasp but such an important one. As I tell my children these words, I have to reflect upon them myself daily as well. Is Jesus the treasure in my life worth giving everything away for? Some days I feel like He is, while some days I see that He is not. Regardless of what I feel, I have to move forward and love

God and our neighbor with all that we have (Matthew 22:35-40) I can't sit around and think back on all my past mistakes and my current shortcomings. I can't make excuses that tomorrow will be the day I start.

We have to dive in head first now and follow Jesus. Yesterday is finished, today is all we have, and tomorrow may never come, so it seems like today is the time for action; today is the time for us to be doers of the Word. St. Peter reminds us about our calling in light of the shortness of life, "The end of all things is at hand. Therefore, be serious and sober for prayers. Above all, let your love for one another be intense, because love covers a multitude of sins" (1 Peter 4: 7-8). The time for us is now. Just think of the billions of lost, poor, and unreached waiting for us to become doers of the word and become Christ for them.

A Self-Examination

As we seek to move deeper into the Glorious Adventure that is our role in the Great Commission, let us ask ourselves a few questions which will hopefully shake us up a bit.

Who is my treasure? What am I treasuring each day and night? Where am I spending most of my time, my money, and my gifts?

Am I madly in love with Jesus Christ, or am I merely following Him out of obligation? While obligation is great and necessary in our Christian life, it is only step one, and we have to move deeper into love. I am obligated to serve my boss or client, but I serve my wife out of love that flows from the deepness of who I am. Jesus wants the latter far more than the former.

Are my passions like Jesus'? Do the poor, lost, and unreached of the world make me come alive? Does loving, serving, and giving my life away for God, my Father, and His people interest me at all?

Am I committed to the Great Commission? Am I taking steps to joining Jesus in going, making disciples, baptizing, and teaching in all nations? Am I committed to or seeking to disciple anyone in my life?

Do I love and serve the poor with joy and gladness? Do I see Christ in the poor and honor the dignity they have? Am I seeking to restore justice and love to the poor around me and even those far from me in the world?

Is the Holy Spirit in charge of my life? Have I ever prayed to the Holy Spirit and given Him control of my life? Or am I still in control of the reigns of my life? In what ways would my life look different if I gave the Holy Spirit control?

Am I a doer of the word or a hearer only? Do my actions match my words and convictions or do I let my convictions slip away to nothing? When is the last time I have acted upon a deep conviction given to me from God? Are there some convictions I need to go back and reclaim and act upon?

Preparing for Jesus

Just like my friend Felipe, we will soon be gathered around by our family and friends and lowered into the earth for our final rest. And at that time, we will have our face to face encounter with Jesus. I am thrilled by that opportunity obviously, but as I read scripture more and more, I also realize that I have been asked to give more and more to Him and those around me before that final encounter occurs. I am deeply inspired by the great saints who died with nearly nothing in their hands, just holding on to Christ. I imagine their encounter with Jesus as they enter paradise for all of eternity.

What will our encounter be like when our life is all said and done and our last breath is taken? What fruit will be blossoming on the tree because of our decision to follow the command of Jesus to *go* and make disciples? I long to hear the words, "Well done, my good and faithful servant . . . come and share your master's joy" (Matthew 25:21). We will enter into eternal paradise and the true Glorious Adventure will begin.

Afterword

If you find yourself desiring to enter more deeply into the Great Commission of Jesus Christ, I encourage you to start at home, but *don't* finish there. Our major issue as Catholics seems to be that we never leave our home. Jesus never commanded us to stay home in the Bible; further he commanded us to leave our homes. Make disciples at home and plan to *go* as Jesus commands us.

Move next to your local Church community and ask your pastor how you can lay down your life to share the Gospel with those in need within your own parish, community, city, or nation. Seek to serve the poor and the lost who need the Gospel in your own community.

Then ask your pastor if your Church can become involved in serving the unreached of the world. There is no limit to the need in our world and close to 3 billion people still need to hear the Gospel of Jesus Christ. Don't be discouraged; while your helping may seem like one small drop in an enormous ocean, it is a very important small drop indeed.

If you sense that your pastor or local Church Parish is not understanding your desire to serve the poor, lost and unreached, that's okay. Don't leave your Church. Just pray that the Holy Spirit would show you avenues to serve the poor, lost, and unreached. As baptized Catholics, we cannot wait for others to lead us into action. We have to be men and women of action. We have to *go* as the Holy Spirit leads us.

If you sense the Holy Spirit moving you to serve among foreign nations, especially the unreached people groups of the world, then don't wait any longer, soon your life will be over. I encourage you to reach out to me at

gloriousadventurethebook@gmail.com or visit
www.familymissionscompany.com. Allow the Holy Spirit to use you in his role of making disciples of all nations.

Endnotes

[1] Francis Chan, "Challenge to the Church," YouTube, November 25, 2013, Video, 4:16. https://www.youtube.com/watch?v=2StRNNnBh4k.

[2] "Nearly Half the World Lives on $5.50 a Day," *World Bank*, October 17, 2018, http://www.worldbank.org/en/news/press-release/2018/10/17/nearly-half-the-world-lives-on-less-than-550-a-day.

[3] "Access to WASH," *Centers for Disease Control and Prevention*, last modified April 11, 2016, https://www.cdc.gov/healthywater/global/wash_statistics.html.

[4] Saint Therese of Lisieux, *Story of a Soul* (Washington: ICS Publications, 1972).

[5] Chris Stefanick, *Contagious Catholicism— The Seven Habits of Modern- day Apostles*, 2006-2016, Lighthouse Talks Agustine Institute, CD-ROM.

[6]The Holy Father Francis, "Evangelii Gaudium," The Holy See, October 8, 2012, vatican.va/evangelii-gaudium/en/files/assets/basic-html/page91.html.

[7] The Holy Father Francis, "Apostolic Exhortation Evangelii Gaudium Of The Holy Father Francis To The Bishops, Clergy, Consecrated Persons And The Lay Faithful On The Proclamation Of The Gospel In Today's World," *The Holy See,* November 24, 2013, http://w2.vatican.va/content/francesco/en/apost_exhortations/documents/papa-francesco_esortazione-ap_20131124_evangelii-gaudium.html.

[8] John Paul II, "15th World Youth Day Address Of The Holy Father John Paul II Vigil Of Prayer," *The Holy See*, last modified August 19, 2000, http://w2.vatican.va/content/john-paul-ii/en/speeches/2000/jul-sep/documents/hf_jp-ii_spe_20000819_gmg-veglia.html.

[9] Saint Augustine of Hippo, *The Confessions of St. Augustine* (Mount Vernon: Peter Pauper Press, 1940-1949).

[10] John Paul II, "Redemptoris Missio," *The Holy See,* December 7, 1990, http://w2.vatican.va/content/john-paul-ii/en/encyclicals/documents/hf_jp-ii_enc_07121990_redemptoris-missio.html.

[11] Thomas Dubay S.M., *Happy Are You Poor* (Denville, NJ: Dimension Books, 1981).

[12] Elisabeth Elliot, *Through the Gates of Splendor* (Carol Stream, IL: Tyndale House, 1975).

[13] *End of the Spear,* directed by Jim Hanon (Chicago: Rocky Mountain Pictures, 2005).

[14] Elisabeth Elliot, *Through the Gates of Splendor* (Carol Stream, IL: Tyndale House, 1975).

[15] Saint Francis de Sales, *Treatise on the Love of God,* trans. Reverend Henry Benedict Mackey O.S.B (London: Aeterna Press, 2015).

[16] Thomas Dubay S.M., *Happy Are You Poor* (Denville, NJ: Dimension Books, 1981).

[17] John Piper, *Let the Nations Be Glad* (Grand Rapids: Baker Publishing Group, 2010).

---

[18] "Thomas Aquinas Quotes," *Goodreads*, accessed November 23, 2019, https://www.brainyquote.com/quotes/thomas_aquinas_192537.

[19] The Holy Father Francis, "Apostolic Exhortation Evangelii Gaudium Of The Holy Father Francis To The Bishops, Clergy, Consecrated Persons And The Lay Faithful On The Proclamation Of The Gospel In Today's World," *The Holy See,* November 24, 2013, http://w2.vatican.va/content/francesco/en/apost_exhortations/documents/papa-francesco_esortazione-ap_20131124_evangelii-gaudium.html.

[20] "Passion," *Dictionary.com*, accessed November 23, 2019. https://www.dictionary.com/browse/passion?s=t.

[21] "Rose of Lima Quote," *AZQuotes*, accessed October 1, 2019, https://www.azquotes.com/quote/607247.

[22] C.S. Lewis, *Mere Christianity* (London: Collins, 1952), 5–56.

[23] John Paul II, "Redemptoris Missio," *The Holy See,* December 7, 1990, http://w2.vatican.va/content/john-paul-ii/en/encyclicals/documents/hf_jp-ii_enc_07121990_redemptoris-missio.html.

[24] *Catechism of the Catholic Church, 2nd ed.* (Washington, DC: United States Catholic Conference, 2000), 842.

[25] *Catechism of the Catholic Church, 2nd ed.* (Washington, DC: United States Catholic Conference, 2000), 614.

[26] John Paul II, "Apostolic Exhortation Familiaris Consortio Of Pope John Paul II To The Episcopate To The Clergy And To The Faithful Of The Whole Catholic Church On The Role Of The

Christian Family In The Modern World," *The Holy See*, November 22, 1981, http://w2.vatican.va/content/john-paul-ii/en/apost_exhortations/documents/hf_jp-ii_exh_19811122_familiaris-consortio.html.

[27] John Paul II, "Redemptoris Missio," *The Holy See,* December 7, 1990, http://w2.vatican.va/content/john-paul-ii/en/encyclicals/documents/hf_jp-ii_enc_07121990_redemptoris-missio.html.

[28] "Prayer of Ignatius of Loyola," *The Prayer Foundation*, accessed November 23, 2019, http://www.prayerfoundation.org/prayer_of_ignatius_of_loyola.htm.

[29] Fred R. Shapiro, "John A. Shedd," in *The Yale Book of Quotations* (New Haven and London: Yale University Press, 2006), 705.

[30] Jonathon and Theresa Kiehl, eulogy.

[31] "St Teresa of Avila." *Our Lady of Mercy*, accessed November 23, 2019, http://olmlaycarmelites.org/quote/teresa-avila?page=2.

[32] Dietrich Bonhoeffer, *The Cost of Discipleship* (New York: Macmillan, 1959), 99.

[33] *Catechism of the Catholic Church, 2nd ed.* (Washington, DC: United States Catholic Conference, 2000), 386.

[34] Philip Yancey, *The Jesus I Never Knew* (Michigan: Zondervan, 1995).

[35] "Mother Teresa Quote," *QuoteDB,* accessed November 23, 2019, quotedb.com/quotes/309.

[36] St. Ambrose, *The Letters of S. Ambrose, Bishop of Milan* (Oxford and Cambridge: The Devonport Society, 1881).

[37] "Caring For The Poor Is Our Passport To Paradise, Says Pope Francis," *Catholic Herald*, November 20, 2017, https://catholicherald.co.uk/news/2017/11/20/care-for-the-poor-says-pope-francis-they-are-your-passport-to-paradise/.

[38] Saint John Chrysostom, *On Wealth and Poverty* (Yonkers, NY: St Vladimirs Seminary Press, 1999), 28.

[39] St. Ambrose, *The Letters of St. Ambrose, Bishop of Milan* (Oxford and Cambridge: The Devonport Society, 1881).

[40] Migne, vol. xiv., col. 747.

[41] Mother Teresa, *Where There is Love There is God* (New York: The Mother Teresa Center, 2010), 337.

[42] "Letter from St Francis Xavier to St Ignatius Loyola," *Independent Catholic News*, December 3, 2014, https://www.indcatholicnews.com/news/26171.

[43] "General Information in Bangladesh," *Joshua Project,* Frontier Ventures, accessed November 23, 2019, https://joshuaproject.net/countries/BG.

[44] "Decree on the Church's Missionary Activity" Vatican II, Ad Gentes Divinitus, December 7, 1965, No. 10.

[45] "Global Statistics," *Joshua Project*, Frontier Ventures, accessed September 3, 2019, https://joshuaproject.net/people_groups/statistics.

[46] "Country: India."*Joshua Project*, Frontier Ventures, accessed

September 3, 2019, http://joshuaproject.net/countries/IN.

[47] "Global Statistics," *Joshua Project*, Frontier Ventures, accessed September 3, 2019, https://joshuaproject.net/people_groups/statistics.

[48] John Paul II, "Redemptoris Missio," *The Holy See,* December 7, 1990, http://w2.vatican.va/content/john-paul-ii/en/encyclicals/documents/hf_jp-ii_enc_07121990_redemptoris-missio.html.

[49] John Paul II, "Redemptoris Missio," *The Holy See,* December 7, 1990, http://w2.vatican.va/content/john-paul-ii/en/encyclicals/documents/hf_jp-ii_enc_07121990_redemptoris-missio.html.

[50] John Paul II, "Redemptoris Missio," *The Holy See,* December 7, 1990, http://w2.vatican.va/content/john-paul-ii/en/encyclicals/documents/hf_jp-ii_enc_07121990_redemptoris-missio.html.

[51] "What is the 10-40 Window?," *Jesus Film Project,* February 18, 2019, https://www.jesusfilm.org/blog-and-stories/10-40-window.html.

[52] John Paul II, "Redemptoris Missio," *The Holy See,* December 7, 1990, http://w2.vatican.va/content/john-paul-ii/en/encyclicals/documents/hf_jp-ii_enc_07121990_redemptoris-missio.html.

[53] "Has Everyone Heard?," *Joshua Project.*, Frontier Ventures, accessed September 3, 2019, http://joshuaproject.net/resources/articles/has_everyone_heard.

[54] "Missions Stats The Current State of the World," *The Traveling Team*, accessed November 23, 2019, http://www.thetravelingteam.org/stats.

[55] "Missions Stats The Current State of the World," *The Traveling Team*, accessed November 23, 2019, http://www.thetravelingteam.org/stats.

[56] Therese of Lisieux," *AZQuotes*, accessed November 23, 2019, https://www.azquotes.com/quote/607245, accessed October 03, 2019.

Made in the USA
Coppell, TX
12 January 2024